CULTURAL POLICY
AND
SOCIALIST FRANCE

CULTURAL POLICY AND SOCIALIST FRANCE

David Wachtel

Contributions in Political Science, Number 177

Greenwood Press
New York • Westport, Connecticut • London

Library of Congress Cataloging-in-Publication Data

Wachtel, David.
    Cultural policy and socialist France.

    (Contributions in political science, ISSN 0147-1066 ;
no. 177)
    Bibliography: p.
    Includes index.
    1. France—Politics and government—1981-
2. France—Cultural policy.   3. Politics and culture—
France—History—20th century.   4. France—Intellectual
life—20th century.   5. Socialism—France—History—
20th century.   I. Title.   II. Series.
DC423.W33   1987   306'.0944   87-285
ISBN 0-313-25549-0 (lib. bdg. : alk. paper)

British Library Cataloguing in Publication Data is available

Library of Congress Catalog Card Number: 87-285
ISBN: 0-313-25549-0
ISSN: 0147-1066

First published in 1987

Greenwood Press, Inc.
88 Post Road West, Westport, Connecticut 06881

Printed in the United States of America

The paper used in this book complies with the
Permanent Paper Standard issued by the National
Information Standards Organization (Z39.48-1984).

10 9 8 7 6 5 4 3 2 1

To my parents,
who have lived with this project as long as I have,
and to the Communauté Miollis,
Où le soleil ne se couche jamais

Contents

Figures and Tables

Preface

This is not a book specifically about art in France in the 1980s.
Rather, it is an attempt to explain and analyze the environment
in which artists and creators worked during the past few years.
It is a book about public policy because the arts in France
depend heavily on government support, and the Socialist party
promised to expand the state role when it was elected in 1981. It
is also a book about politics because culture became a major
political issue in the 1980s. Finally, it is a book about
society because the basis for a cultural policy and the emergence
of a cultural debate in the 1980s belongs, in part, to the
changing needs and preoccupations of the French public and its
political leadership.

This book is the product of many years of research. I began
studying Jack Lang and the French Socialists' cultural policy in
Paris in 1983. As it turned out, I arrived at a critical moment.
The ideological fervor of the cultural policy had reached its
peak, and the ministry was attacked from many directions. Since
then, as I explored further contemporary French history,
politics, and society, I was struck by the way in which so many
diverse areas touched on culture. The story of cultural policy
and the politics surrounding it, I realized, was a microcosm of
much of the Socialist experience.

There is good reason to believe that France is passing
through an important decade of political and social transition.
The controversy surrounding culture during the past few years is
an important reflection of it.

This book is not just about France, however. The issue of
cultural policy itself is of equal importance. Since ancient
times, societies have been faced with questions of how to support
the arts and artists as well as preserve a cultural heritage. In
modern times, government has assumed an increasingly important
role in the arts. The diversity of experience is tremendous, and
there is always room for improvement. France has proved to be a
useful laboratory of arts management during the past few years--
and we can all learn from her successes and mistakes.

Acknowledgments

I would like to thank the many people whose cooperation made this book possible. First, I wish to mention the many interview subjects in France who, by sharing their thoughts and experience, brought "la politique culturelle" to life--particularly Jack Lang and the members of his cabinet, Guy de Brebisson of the Ministry's Service des Etudes et Recherches, Jean Musy of the City of Paris Direction of Cultural Affairs, Jacques Rigaud, and Pierre Boulez. Through their thoughts and boundless activity, these people and the many others who work with them are proof that French culture will be well served in the future.

I also would like to thank the many friends whose support was critical. Dr. and Mrs. Frank Katz gave up their home and computer during the writing stage, and my friend Philippe Cristelli sacrificed his apartment and telephone while I did research in Paris. Other friends whose advice, support, and friendship made this American feel at home in Paris are Isabelle Mounier-Kuhn, Catherine Chalin, Philippe Aguera, Jean-Michel Casa and Isabella Palumbo-Fossati, Laurence and Dominique Monneron, Tim Stevens, Taiko Takahashi, and Stéphane Pallez.

Since this project first began as my senior thesis at Princeton three years ago, I relied on the advice and help of numerous faculty members. Thanks are in order for my first advisor, Nancy Bermeo, as well as for Lynn White III of the Woodrow Wilson School. Nicholas Wahl, director of NYU's Institute of French Studies, was helpful in providing me introductions during my second stay in Paris in 1986.

Finally, I would like to make special mention of André Maman of Princeton's Romance Languages Department. Professor Maman first introduced me to the study of France six years ago, and I am permanently indebted to him. His work and love for France are an inspiration to all of his students.

French Terms and Abbreviations

Adjoints chargés des affaires culturelles: municipal cultural aides

ADMICAL (Association pour le Développement du Mécénat Industriel et Commercial): private group that promotes corporate sponsorship of the arts

Antenne 2: state TV channel

Arthothèque: art lending library

CAC (Centre d'Action Culturelle): municipal cultural center; differs from a Maison de la Culture only in source of funding

Cahiers des charges: licensing regulations and programing requirements issued by the government to all television stations

Canal plus: pay-television station; established 1984

CGT (Confédération Générale du Travail): Communist-dominated trade union

CNAP (Centre National des Arts Plastiques): administrative and financial unit of Delegation of Plastic Arts

DRAC (Directeur Régional d'Action Culturel): representative of the Ministry of Culture in each region. Chief administrator of most decentralization initiatives

ENA (Ecole Nationale d'Administration): national school of public administration

Enarque: graduate of ENA

FEN (Fédération de l'Education Nationale): Socialist-dominated teachers' union

FNAC (Fédération Nationale d'Achat de Cadres): leading French book, audio, and photographic retailer

FIACRE (Fonds d'Incitation à la Création): special fund set up by the Delegation of Plastic Arts to finance individual artists and projects

FRAC (Fonds Régionaux d'Art Contemporain): contemporary art acquisition program funded jointly by the Ministry of Culture and each of France's twenty-two regions

FR3 (France Régional 3): French regional TV network

Grandes écoles: France's elite university-level schools: ENA, Polytéchnique, Ecole des Mines, Ecole des Ponts et Chausées.

Grands projets: the large construction/cultural projects in Paris sponsored by President Mitterrand--the Bastille Opera, Grand Louvre, Institut du Monde Arab, Musée d'Orsay, La Villette (science and technical museum and music conservatory), Ministry of Finance at Bercy, and Tête de la Défense

IRCAM (Institut de Recherche et Coordination Acoustique/Musique): Contemporary music research and composition center located within Paris' Pompidou Center.

Loi Lang: book law that set prices within a 5 percent margin of publishers' list.

Maison de la Culture: cultural center; focus of Malraux's cultural policy.

Mécénat: private patronage of the arts.

ORTF (Office de la Radio et Télévision Francaise): agency that controlled all French domestic broadcasting until 1974

PCF (Parti Communiste Francais): French Communist party

PS (Parti Socialiste): French Socialist party, founded 1971

PSU (Parti Socialiste Unifié): Socialist group that merged with the PS in 1971

Radio libre: private, FM radio station

RPR (Rassemblement pour la République): Gaullist party led by Jacques Chirac

RTL (Radio-Télévision Luxembourg): Private Luxembourg TV station, broadcasting in French, that can be seen in much of eastern France.

SEPT (Société Européene de Production de Télévision): Television production company.

SFIO (Section Francaise de l'Internationale Ouvrière): French socialist party during the Third and Fourth Republics

SFP (Société Francaise de Production): Entity once responsible for all French television programing.

SOFICA (Sociétés de financement des Industries Cinématographiques et Audiovisuelles): New film production tax shelters.

TF1 (Télévision Francaise 1): Oldest and largest television station. Formerly state-owned, but privatized in 1987

TNP: Théâtre National Populaire.

UDF (Union des Democrats Francais): Giscardian party.

CULTURAL POLICY
AND
SOCIALIST FRANCE

Introduction
The Politics of Culture

> C'est bien en cela d'ailleurs que la structure d'une
> culture, faite des symboles valorisés, est beaucoup plus
> difficile à analyser qu'un langage.*
>
> Lucien Goldmann, <u>La Création Culturelle dans la Société
> Moderne</u>

On July 5, 1983, French President Francois Mitterrand announced
the cancellation of a popular exhibition in Paris scheduled for
the 1989 bicentennial of the French Revolution. The president
declared that the 2-billion-dollar spectacle would not take place
because Paris Mayor Jacques Chirac refused to cooperate. What
followed was a political sparring match between President
Mitterrand, France's first socialist head of state in twenty-
three years, and Chirac, his principal opponent and the man who,
ironically, would become his prime minister in 1986. Chirac
maintained that the price tag was too high, especially in a
period of austerity, but most of the press agreed that, at least
for the short term, Mitterrand had won the latest round. Even if
the exhibition had become a white elephant, as many critics
believed, the blame for its failure effectively had been pinned
on the mayor.

The cancellation of Expo '89 was, however, a serious
symbolic blow to France's socialist government. Past <u>Expositions
Universelles</u> did much to advance French pride and international
prestige and often left the country with impressive monuments.
The Eiffel Tower was erected for the centennial exposition in
1889. The first Metro lines were inaugurated in time for the
1900 fair. The Socialists were hoping that their expo would
become a celebration not only of 1789 but also of a new and
dynamic French culture, a celebration of seven years of socialist
achievement. Perhaps for this reason, many of the expensive
building projects originally designed to highlight the expo--from

---

* It is because of this, then, that the structure of a culture,
made up of valued symbols, is more difficult to analyze than a
language.

a rock concert hall to a new "popular" opera house--continued on schedule.

In many countries, cancellation of a cultural event, no matter how large, would have few grave repercussions. Not so in France.   The death of Expo '89 marked the beginning of a major challenge to the government and a symbolic end to an ideological commitment that the Socialist party was no longer able to manage. Henceforth, many of the lofty, ideological goals of the Socialist cultural policy would have to be pared in much the same way that pragmatic rigeur had overtaken earlier dreams of economic expansion.

The first signs of trouble came in March 1983, when the Socialists suffered severe losses in municipal elections.   While the setbacks reflected public disenchantment with the state of the economy and government policies in general, many mayoral campaigns were characterized by bitter debates over the government's extensive cultural policies.   Attention was focused on the role of the Maisons de la Culture and other cultural centers and programs.   The Socialists claimed that they sought to reach a new public through innovative programs and contemporary (often avant-garde) productions; the Right charged that the entire cultural apparatus was controlled by Leftists who used it for political purposes and produced nothing of interest to local audiences.   Opposition attacks on "socialist culture" continued into the summer and culminated with a well-coordinated "assault" on the Maisons de la Culture by newly elected mayors in early July.   Scores of employees were fired as the Right sought to flex its muscles in an area traditionally considered the terrain of the Left.   Throughout the entire period, France's normally vocal intellectual community maintained an eerie silence that disturbed Socialist leaders who had counted the community among their strongest allies.

On July 8, the lead headline in Le Monde read "The Future of the Left and the Cultural Battle."   The Socialists, said Le Monde, had some reasons to be upset about the latest "counteroffensive" of the Right:

> The socialists had perhaps believed that the culture which
> they represent, and with which they have slowly impregnated
> the country, would impose itself by the magic of power. The
> socialists are, on the contrary, more than ever in a
> defensive situation.   Some speak of "cultural resistance."
> The expression, as dramatic as it sounds, describes an
> evolution which no one would have believed possible two
> years ago. (1)

Once backed into a corner, the ministry's response was swift.   An administrative housecleaning, emphasizing tighter management and fiscal controls, was implemented.   Meanwhile, Minister of Culture Jack Lang, the greatest "communicator" to hold the job since de Gaulle created the post for writer André Malraux, dropped much of the ideological tone that characterized his first two years in office and set off on a campaign to promote himself and his vision of culture. His call for cultural diversity, a link between culture and economic rejuvenation, and a break with stuffy, classical definitions of culture struck an important chord with the public. By the time the March 1986 legislative elections took place, polls showed that Lang was the most popular minister, and the public seemed to endorse his policies. Voters rejected the Socialist party, but few were opposed to the cultural path it had charted for the nation.

Few American observers realize how important culture is to France's Socialist party. Economic issues are well publicized abroad, but cultural questions are either ignored or joked about. Lang raised a few eyebrows at a UNESCO conference in Mexico in 1982 when he called for a crusade against "American cultural imperialism." One year later, Lang again made front pages throughout the world by inviting hundreds of well-known intellectuals (mostly Left-leaning) to the Sorbonne for a "Creation and Development" colloquium dedicated to "cultural solutions to the world economic crisis." Though a full-fledged member of the cabinet at the time, Lang officially had no authority in foreign affairs (the Quai D'Orsay is responsible for external cultural relations), and the international "crusade" backfired. The intellectual community did not go along with it, and the government eventually found Lang's anti-American outbursts (such as refusing to attend the annual American Film Festival in Deauville) to be embarrassing. Nevertheless, the minister did succeed, through trips to Cuba, critiques of "Dallas" and warm welcomes for dissident intellectuals, (2) in projecting a new image of France as an independent-minded cultural leader.

American journalists in particular found Lang to be a typical example of French chauvinism--the perfect subject for ridicule. Few bothered to look beyond the headline-catching statements and examine what Lang actually was accomplishing at home. Between 1981 and 1986, the long neglected Ministry of Culture grew to encompass 13,000 employees managing a budget of about one-billion dollars. The budget, double the amount spent during President Valéry Giscard D'Estaing's last year in office, does not include the larger local government expenditure on culture, often spearheaded by Socialist municipalities and indirectly influenced by the ministry through its use of cofinancing and loans of technical expertise. (3) Even during the last years of economic retrenchment, cultural spending on the national and local levels continued to increase.

The Socialist preoccupation with culture is not unique to the Mitterrand government or even to France. Socialists in Europe have long looked to the intellectual community and cultural institutions as a source of support and legitimacy. Historically, intellectuals have been attracted to parties of the Left, and many have played active political roles. More recently, as socialists in southern Europe--Spain and Greece as well as France--spent many years out of power, wedged between Rightist majorities on one side and communist parties on the other, they came to see cultural affairs as a medium for quietly promoting new ideas and social change, a stepping-stone to eventual success in the political arena.

Since coming to power in the early 1980s, the "southern socialists" were faced with questions of implementing highly

ideological policies on national and international   levels.
Strong cultural constituencies that grew up during the opposition
years   found that their demands must compete with other   pressing
issues.   The   intense nationalism that often surrounded the   new
socialist   cultural   policies also created difficulties   abroad.
The   heavy inroads made by American popular culture in Europe   in
recent   years--from movies to music to fast food--are sources   of
deep   concern   and   embarrassment for many European socialists.
Over time, socialist policymakers have learned that broad attacks
on the problem will not make it go away.   If they wish to revive
interest   in   their   own national   cultures,   they   must   develop
innovative   policies   that will make   the   public   respond.   The
French   Socialists'   slow   realization   of this   fact   and   their
attempts to do something about it were critical elements   shaping
cultural policy in the early 1980s.
     The   decision to analyze only one country's cultural   policy
comes   for a number of reasons.   First is the historic role that
the   French state has carved out for itself in cultural   affairs.
Louis   XIV   gave the first subsidy to the   Comédie Francaise   in
1682.   Since   the   1950s,   the democratic Fifth Republic has
developed   an elaborate system of direct and indirect   government
support that underwrites nearly every aspect of national cultural
life.   Theaters, museums, and regional Maisons de la Culture are
written into the budget; taxes on movie tickets are   used   to
subsidize production and export of new films;   the price of books
is   regulated and television was,   until recently,   a government
monopoly.   Most   of   this   was   accomplished by Gaullist   and
conservative   governments with bipartisan support.   The   French
Socialists   thus   inherited   a   well-developed   administrative
structure into which they poured large amounts of money and, they
claimed, a new set of priorities.
     A   second   reason   to focus on France is the   nature   of   the
Parti Socialiste (PS) itself.   The Socialist leadership has been
committed   personally to a policy of cultural transformation   for
more   than a decade.   In France,   the socialist movement
traditionally has been a magnet for intellectuals and   educators.
Turn-of-the-century socialists such as Jean Jaurès led the fight
for   public   education.   Léon Blum's Popular Front government
initiated   the country's first modern social and economic reforms
in the 1930s.   Mitterrand and his colleagues assembled a similar
coalition in the 1970s with the justification that France   needed
a   cultural transformation to break down the "elitist" nature   of
French   society   and open the way for other social reforms and   a
creative   awakening.   Culture was no longer a side issue but
a central political objective.   As the 1981 electoral   platform
states, "For the socialists culture is not the privilege of a few
institutions or places.   This is to say that the achievement   of
our   cultural   goals   goes   together   with   all   of   the   social
transformations that are part of the Projet Socialiste. (4)
     The party platform was not meant as an empty   promise.   The
"culture   project," as the PS came to call it,   evolved over more
than a decade prior to Mitterrand's presidential victory in 1981.
A   concerted   effort began to promote cultural activities,   or
action culturelle, in municipalities under Socialist control
throughout the 1970s.   Coinciding with a decreased interest in

cultural spending by the Giscard government, the PS's emphasis on culture gained the party widespread support and was an important factor in the 1981 victory. The powerful artistic and intellectual communities interpreted the socialist commitment to culture as a sign of the party's commitment to them. Meanwhile, the politicians realized that the policies also responded to the needs of the general population in the provinces as well. After two decades of unprecedented economic growth, society had more resources, education, and leisure time to spend on cultural activities than ever before.

A final reason to choose France is the allure of French culture itself in the world community. Perhaps no other country has had such a disproportionate influence on Western culture. France still commands a great deal of respect as a leader in the arts despite the fact that many leaders of both the Left and Right share the belief that French culture has been in a marked state of decline at home and abroad for many years. The PS came to power determined to arrest that decline through government action. With much fanfare, spending was increased dramatically, and, most important, the ministry greatly expanded its domain. According to Lang, "Culture is a large and generous concept. . . Culture is all of you in all your daily acts." (5) Lang's flexible definition of culture enabled the ministry to extend recognition and funding to a range of new areas--jazz, fashion, comic books, and video technology--and was a major factor behind increased public support for the cultural policies.

The question still remains, however, as to what the Socialists' ultimate objectives were. The popular perception is that, if anything, the PS scored a major public relations coup. This was not, however, the sole intention of the men who shaped the cultural policy and is even farther away from the theories that guided them. President Mitterrand and some of his closest associates, such as Councilor Jacques Attali, were fond of saying that "socialism is, first of all, a cultural project." (6) What have they achieved after five years? Why did they gamble so much on culture?

This study takes the form of a multifaceted approach to understanding and evaluating the policies of the French Ministry of Culture under Mitterrand and Lang. It assumes that there has been a major evolution in French society and the way it views culture over the past fifteen years, and it seeks to determine what role the Socialist party had in that change. An earlier study of politics and culture in France would almost certainly have focused primarily on the French Communist party. Today, the Parti Communiste Francais (PCF) has lost almost all of its intellectual support, and while Communist municipalities spend large amounts of money on culture in what appears to be a fairly concerted effort, the party itself has played a minor role in shaping national cultural policy since the 1960s. It was never accepted as an alternative by the members of what cultural historian Pascal Ory terms the <u>tiers état culturel</u>, the disaffected students of 1968 and the neglected provincial political and cultural leaders whom the Socialists successfully united. (7)

For students of the French Left, culture is one of the more dramatic examples of the Socialists' ability under Mitterrand's leadership to relegate the Communists to a secondary position. In terms of influence and policy, the PS successfully stole cultural legitimacy away from the PCF in little more than a decade; and, by so doing, the Socialists could claim culture as a basis, albeit fragile, for their own political legitimacy as well.

It is tempting to bury a topic such as this under a mountain of ethical issues, but that is not the intention of this study. Rather, it will seek to analyze and comment upon the development and implementation of public policy by a socialist party within the constructs of a liberal-democratic society.

The early chapters of this study are meant to explore how culture came to be seen as a source of political legitimation by French socialists. Chapter 1, "Culture and the Search for Political Legitimation in France," details the origins of Socialist cultural policy from a theoretical angle. The ideas of leading socialist thinkers and their influence on political and institutional developments during the Third and Fifth republics are considered. Of equal importance is the important role of leading French intellectuals in cultural affairs. Chapter 2, "The Road to 1981," explains the place of cultural affairs in the evolution of the PS. The chapter looks at party membership and the use of culture by newly elected Socialist mayors and municipal councils throughout the 1970s. The Socialist "cultural project" was essentially conceived at the local level, so the Lang ministry's mixed commitment to decentralization after 1981, the final topic discussed, is of particular interest.

The later chapters concentrate on the development of Socialist cultural policy between 1981 and 1986. Chapter 3, "Political Culture and Cultural Policy," breaks the period into two parts and then looks at government support of theater, museums, music, art, the cultural industries, and corporate patronage. The focus is on individual policy initiatives and their place in the legitimation process, if any. Chapters 4 and 5 adopt a similar format to examine two areas with a close relation to cultural policy: broadcasting and architecture. Chapter 6, "The End of the Monopoly," looks at how Socialist command over cultural issues--and thus, to a certain extent, the party's own political legitimacy--came under increasing attack after 1981. The use of culture as an electoral issue by both Left and Right, first in the 1983 municipal vote and later in the 1986 legislative contest, is of primary interest.

The conclusion relates the experience of the past few years to the questions posed in the early chapters and examines the relationship between culture and political legitimation in the objectives of the French Socialists. It also examines the larger implications of the Lang years for French culture and for American cultural interests as well.

NOTES

1. Jean-Yves Lhomeau, "L'Avenir de la Gauche et la Bataille Culturelle," Le Monde, July 8, 1983, p. 1. All translations by author unless otherwise noted.

2. One of Mitterrand's first acts as president was to grant French citizenship to Argentine author Julio Cortazar. Leading foreign filmmakers invited to live and work in France include Costa Gavras (Greece), Yilmaz Gurney (Turkey), and Andres Wajda (Poland).

3. A frequent problem for researchers in the cultural area is the lack of comparative statistics for determining how much money various nations spend on culture, here broadly defined as including anything pertaining to education, presentation, and practice of the arts. Each nation measures expenditures differently. Cultural responsibilities often are split between many ministries or departments. Also, depending upon the degree of centralization in a given country, culture is sometimes the responsibility of local, not national, governments. A comparative study prepared for the National Endowment for the Arts in 1978 showed the following results: France ($11.88 per capita/.667 percent of national budget), Great Britain ($3.60/.173 percent), United States ($1.61/.068 percent). Television was not included, except for public television in the United States. (Cecilia C. Kasavitch, "A Brief Comparison of Spending on the Arts," prepared for the National Endowment for the Arts, Washington, D.C., December 22, 1978.)

4. Projet Socialiste Pour les Années 80 (Paris: Club Socialiste du Livre, 1981), p. 281.

5. Jack Lang, address to UNESCO conference in Mexico City, July 27, 1982.

6. "L'enjeu de Société n'est pas Politique, Mais Culturel, déclare M. Jacques Attali," Le Monde, May 21, 1981, p. 16. John Vinocur, "Will French Culture Be More French?" New York Times, January 9, 1983, sec. 2, p. 1.

7. Pascal Ory, L'entre-deux mai (Paris: Editions du Seuil, 1983), p. 14.

1
Culture and the Search for Political Legitimation in France

Le citoyen réplique en contestant la légitimité culturelle de l'autorité civile en tant que gouvernement. Il place la legitimité culturelle dans une idéologie politique qui, si elle était adoptée par le gouvernement, ou si le parti devenait le gouvernement, lui donnerait enfin la légitimité culturelle et la dignité d'Etat.*

Jesse R. Pitts, "Les Francais et l'Autorité," <u>Francais, Qui Etes-Vous?</u>

Despite three decades of unparalleled social and economic progress, France in 1981 remained a nation of contrasts. Income disparity was among the highest in Western Europe; the two-tiered education system of prestigious Grandes Ecoles and overcrowded, underfunded universities was notoriously unfair; and a political, social, and mental gulf separated Paris from the provinces more than any geographic barrier. These contrasts created a powerful elite, removed from most ordinary citizens.

Because of the nature of this elite, change does not come easily to France. Those who have sought to challenge the system never have been able to do so from the outside. French Socialists have generally operated under this assumption since Jean Jaurès took control of the Parti Socialiste Unifié(PSU) in 1905. According to George A. Codding Jr., "It was [Jaurès's] concept--that social reforms could provide the way for the coming of socialism to which all socialists should direct their efforts--that became the accepted doctrine of the unified party. (1) For Jaurès, the decisive factor of social progress of the Third Republic was its policy of implementing a lay public

---

* The citizen replies by questioning the cultural legitimacy of the civilian authority as a government. He places cultural legitimacy within a political ideology that, if adopted by the government, or if the party became the government, would give it cultural legitimacy and the dignity of the State.

education system during the 1880s and 1890s. "Lay teaching, social progress, they are two indivisible formulas," he said. (2)

Nearly six decades after Jaurès's assassination, a new generation of socialists, following in the shadow of their founder's doctrine, replaced education with a new concept of social progress, _action culturelle_, a loose collection of ideas and institutions that fostered cultural awareness and creativity as a means of effecting social change. The new Socialist concept of culture was that of a liberating force--one that blurred the distinction between creator and spectator, that separated art and innovation from the profit motive. Mitterrand wrote at the outset of his 1974 presidential campaign:

> _Action culturelle_ cannot substitute for political action since it supposes deep economic changes. It should not be, however, a "soul soother" destined to make the present segregation and injustices tolerable. This is why I see it tied in every way to the transformation of the social order. The two movements are neither competitive nor identical, they complete each other. (3)

Much of the impetus behind _action culturelle_ came from the debate that preceded the May 1968 riots in France. Pierre Gaudibert writes that "beginning in the 1960s, the idea slowly emerged that _action culturelle_, backed by the state, was capable of causing a 'mutation' in national life more profound than anything since the system of public education was put in place between 1880 and 1890." (4)

A successful socialist cultural policy would represent a significant reform. French social scientists have long been convinced that social distinctions in France are tied to cultural differences. Charles Maier notes that the French bourgeois elite relied foremost on "aesthetic snobbism" in its successful attempt to reestablish the social order after World War I. As an example of the trend toward cultural elitism, he cites the debate surrounding the initiative of Léon Berard, minister of education from 1922 to 1924, to tighten up classical education requirements for the baccalauréat:

> Berard claimed that he was merely trying to reinforce national values, "but under the simple pedagogical question," wrote the sensitive commentator Edmund Goblot, "there is the question of social class. . . The bourgeois needs a culture that differentiates an elite. . . a culture deluxe." (5)

During the 1960s, empirical social research in France strongly supported earlier arguments of cultural elitism. Landmark studies such as _Les Héritiers_ by sociologists Pierre Bourdieu and Jean-Claude Passeron clearly demonstrated that success at the universities was linked to cultural levels, thus favoring upper- and middle-class students. Social and economic approaches to creation and consumption of culture also can be found in Raymonde Moulin's studies of the art market in France and Pierre-Michel Menger's works on music. (6)

Thus, The precedent for viewing culture as part of a larger social and economic problem was well established by the early 1970s, just as the reconstituted PS was seeking fresh ideas for creating peaceful change in France. The issue became how to move "from an elitist concept of culture to a popular one." (7) According to a report of policy recommendations drawn up during the first months of the Mitterrand administration for the Ministry of Culture, "Action culturelle, maintaining that cultures awaken consciousness, is a source of dignity and helps one reject submission." (8)

INTELLECTUALS, THE LEFT, AND THE STATE

In reality, French Socialists had been confronting the issue of cultural elitism long before Mitterrand and his advisors, swept up in the passions of 1968, adopted the issue. "Throughout the centuries," wrote Jaurès in 1894, "man could only aspire to justice by aspiring for a social order, less contradictory to man than the present order, and prepared by the present order." (9)
By the turn of the century, a significant group of Leftist intellectuals was no longer content to remain "poets on the barricades" as F. W. J. Hemmings chooses to describe their nineteenth-century revolutionary counterparts. The Dreyfus Affair, the celebrated fin de siècle case of a Jewish army captain who was unjustly accused of treason and railroaded into jail by a military court, split French society apart and nearly brought down the republic. At the same time, it marked the entrance of the intellectual community into political life. Author Emile Zola launched his famous "J'accuse" editorial in Le Figaro in defense of Dreyfus in what became a rallying cry for intellectuals to join en masse in the political debate. While some artists had been active in political life throughout the nineteenth century, most often they had acted as individual citizens. "J'accuse" and the passions it engendered on both sides brought the idea of a cultural cause directly into politics, a factor that would be brought up again and again during the multiple political crises of the twentieth century, from the "Affaire" to the Popular Front, the Liberation, the return of de Gaulle to establish the Fifth Republic, and May 1968. With a few important exceptions, the intellectual community identified itself with the "forces of progress" on France's divided Left. (10)
Although many intellectuals and artists from Aragon to Sartre became identified with the Communist party, it is important to recognize that the allegiance of most intellectuals was never tied permanently. Following the schism between the Section Francaise de l'Internationale Ouvrière (SFIO) and Communists in 1920, the socialists were free to develop their own French interpreters of Marx. (11) This factor was crucial in permitting generations of socialist intellectuals not only to articulate ideas for nonrevolutionary social change, but also to influence policy and build institutions during periods when the SFIO took part in government. The interplay of ideas with policy has largely eluded French Communists, but it is an essential part

of France's socialist heritage.

Jaurès's support for public education and his desire for a new order "prepared by the present order" promoted the idea that political power was only a means to an end--that of a new society--and not an end in itself. Léon Blum, Jaurès's spiritual and political heir as head of the post-World War I SFIO, became the first socialist to have the opportunity to translate this principle into political action. In a 1919 speech to a Socialist Party National Congress, Blum stated:

> The party is in evolution, in constant movement between two points, two fixed polls: one is the future society which we foresee, which we predict, which we want to realize; the other is the present society, out of which we want to carve that future society. We have, so to speak, one foot in the real and one in the ideal. (12)

As head of the Popular Front government in 1936, Blum was responsible for implementing the country's first modern social, economic, and cultural reforms.

Blum's approach to politics was based on a combination of ideology and pragmatism that saw political power as "necessary but not sufficient" for attaining social transformation. He instead envisioned a long period of "continuous evolution," and he acknowledged the fact that "the action of a small group might work in Russia, but not in the West." (13) The objectives of any socialist participation in the Third Republic, he believed, would be to pass some of the measures that would prepare the way for the eventual transformation of society.

Blum, a former literary critic, once wrote that the proletariat must have economic needs met but also "all the pleasures of culture, all the pleasures of art." (14) In his short term in office (less than two years), he worked to create an agenda of social and cultural reforms that left its imprint on France for decades. The Popular Front was guided by the idea that culture was not just for an elite, that everyone had a "right to rest and leisure." Fundamental to this right was the belief that a breakdown of elitism in culture was part of the general transformation of society that the socialists dreamed of. Cultural reform represented, in effect, a perfect case of Blum's keeping "one foot in the real and one in the ideal." An article in the socialist journal *Vendredi* in 1936 noted,

> Parallel to the great political and social movement of the Popular Front. . . a vast cultural movement is taking place. Its motto ought to be: Let us open the gates of culture. Let us scale the wall that surrounds like a beautiful park, closed to the poor, a culture reserved for a privileged elite. (15)

The most tangible results of the Popular Front's cultural policy were contained within the Matignon labor accords of 1936 and included the stipulation of a forty-hour work week and the first guaranteed paid-vacation periods. With the encouragement of Cabinet Secretary Leo Lagrange, workers and youths traveled throughout France in the summer of 1936 in unprecedented numbers. "Sport, tourism, and culture are not new pleasures in our modern civilization," wrote Lagrange in July 1936. "They have, however, become with rare exceptions the privilege of one social class the means to practice sports and tourism and to know the joys of culture." (16) Culture was popularized to some degree in many countries during the 1930s, but Lagrange's comment reveals the unique approach of the French Socialists--the goal of self-realization. This was, of course, in great contrast to Hitler's Aryan Man or Stalin's New Soviet Man, the embodiment of realization for the state. (17) Neither was the Popular Front's cultural effort matched by Roosevelt's New Deal since the Federal Theater Project and related WPA programs were conceived of as projects for the unemployed rather than as programs to help the arts as such.

Perhaps the most important contribution of the Popular Front's cultural policies was not the Matignon labor accords but rather the ambitious ideas advanced by people such as Lagrange and Blum but never acted upon: decentralization, provincial arts festivals, Maisons de la Culture, and reform of the national theaters such as the Comédie Francaise. These ideas continue to be relevant to this day, especially for Mitterrand's Socialists, who consider themselves to be spiritual heirs to the Popular Front. Neither have they remained dormant during the interim. After the years of war and postwar rebuilding, they were brought back to center stage under unusual conditions by André Malraux when General de Gaulle installed the writer/intellectual as France's first minister of culture in 1959.

A humanist intellectual and sometime revolutionary (in 1920s China and Republican Spain), Malraux shared many ideas on culture with the Popular Front and earlier socialists. The cornerstone of his policy was the "democratization of culture" in the form of the Maisons de la Culture, centers designed to distribute the arts throughout the country, to all levels of the population. The goal was to place one Maison de la Culture (with museums, theater companies, and such) each of France's ninety-five departments, with budgets split fifty-fifty between the ministry and local authorities. Malraux told the National Assembly in 1966, "We must, in a way, be sure that each child in France can have the right to paintings, to theater, to cinema, just the same as the child's right to the alphabet." (18)

Malraux's entire cultural program met with suspicion among conservatives, many of whom viewed the Maisons de la Culture as refuges for Leftists and Leftist ideas. Pierre Cabanne notes, "For some, even at the Elysée, the minister/writer was the heir to the Popular Front, and the 'democratization of culture,' only a variant of its egalitarian ideology." (19) For those who question the whole idea of a Ministry of Culture, Malraux is more vilified than any socialist, from Blum to Lang, because of his ability to convince the Right and Center of the Leftist "myth" of state patronage, by combining the jacobine tradition of the Left with the Right's traditional notions of nationalism as expounded by writer Charles Maurras and embraced by de Gaulle. (20) Malraux was captivated by the Gaullist notion of national unity. A shared, common culture, free of elitist strands, was, for him, a "force for union," part of the "unifying myth." (21)   He once explained to the <u>Nouvel Observateur</u>, "I replaced [the notion of] the proletariat for [that of] France." (22)   However, by abandoning the idea of transforming society in favor of the Gaullist vision of using politics to overcome class divisions, Malraux gained acceptance on the Right, but also surprising animosity on the Left, which often charged him with turning the ministry into a shopwindow of French culture rather than an active force.   His troubles were compounded further by the lack of financial support he received, a factor which most artists hold against him to this day.

Malraux's contribution to the growth of socialist concepts of culture is thus a topic that sparks much debate on the Left. According to Mitterrand, "Malraux's acts did not always follow the direction of his thought." (23)   The Maisons de la Culture never attained the primary role in French society that Malraux envisioned (only fourteen were built), but they represented the first attempt to institutionalize the socialist concept of cultural equality and democratization of culture. For many, however, the politics and bureaucracy of these "egalitarian" institutions turned the ministry into a new kind of hegemony, behind which stood a repressive, narrow Gaullist concept of society. In a 1968 pamphlet entitled <u>Asphyxiating Culture</u>, painter Dubuffet decried "the word culture [being] associated with an entire structure (<u>appareil</u>) of intimidation and pressure." (24)   The writer Catherine Clément, a leading PS cultural militant, notes,

> The revolutionary had become a conformist. . . . To be a conformist is to restrain our heritage to the most secure values and refuse anything which appears to threaten them. It is, however, often that which threatens directly that leads us to the surest creation. (25)

MAY 1968: A TURNING POINT

Within the Socialist critique of Malraux lay the seeds of intellectual support for the 1968 protests: the rejection of "stifling" institutions and support for a more active, provocative culture. The two weeks of student and worker strikes that shook the entire country represented an important opportunity to revise the Left's theory of culture.

Perhaps the most interesting new theories to be grafted onto the French experience were discovered in the writings of Italian philosopher Antonio Gramsci (1891-1937), one of the spiritual fathers of Italy's remarkably independent Communist party. Although they had no direct influence on French contemporaries, Gramsci's writings address many of the same dilemmas that socialist leaders after Jaurès confronted, namely, the desire for "humanism" as the basis for a new socialist culture and the inapplicability of the Russian experience to the West.

As the socialists began to reorganize themselves after the political debacle of 1968, Gramsci's writings drew increasing attention because they introduced concepts of institutional structure, ideology, education, and culture--themes long advocated by the French Left--to complement the heavy emphasis of earlier Marxist economic thought on the conditions for creating social change. Jacques Texier, an early Gramsci scholar, told a colloquium in Rome in 1969 of the "essential fact that for the first time Gramsci's thought has found an entrance to insert itself in the deep controversies that animate ideological life in France." (26) French academics who wrote extensively on Gramsci during the late 1960s include Jean-Marc Piotte, Hugues Portelli and Christine Buci Glucksmann.

Like many European socialists after World War I, Gramsci was concerned about the future role of socialism in the so-called "bourgeois" states. Most socialist parties supported their national war efforts, despite some misgivings. In France and Italy, they had even agreed to enter the governments. The doctrine of revolution was shed as a result of wartime nationalist feeling and a postwar realization that Western European states, unlike Czarist Russia, were too well established to permit a rapid political turnover. Gramsci set about redefining the nature of political power in the West--emphasizing the strength of civil society over government authority--and thus developed a new theory of socialist revolution. Gramsci's "war of position," a blueprint for Western socialists and Eurocommunists, is essentially a fight for hegemony, a condition of ideological, cultural, and political dominance that is separate from actual political power. According to Gramsci, hegemonic power determines the true ruling class, not control of the government, which is only a later by-product. The bourgeoisie became the ruling class because they had succeeded in creating an "organically integrated society," by consensus rather than by force, and had thus been able to shape all social, cultural, legal, and political institutions. (27) The "war of position" calls for significant intellectual and cultural reforms. The idea is for the working class to develop its own independent culture and autonomous intellectual class, challenging and superseding the foundations of bourgeois hegemony.

Certain aspects of Gramsci's thoughts on culture and society are of particular interest in light of developments in French intellectual thinking since 1968. First is the role of the intellectual. Leonardo Salamini writes that both Piotte and Portelli, two of the leading French commentators on Gramsci, share the perspective of the centrality of the role of intellectuals and notes that "this concept. . . sets Gramsci apart from Marx and Lenin, and is rich in practical consequences for socialist transformation in Western societies." (28) The new "organic" intellectual, belonging to the working class and working with it, was seen as paramount in lifting proletarian consciousness. (29) The interpretations of Piotte and Portelli went beyond the theoretical realm, however, and are reflected in the attitudes of many French artists. In his 1973 study of French society, John Ardagh described cultural progress as being "sabotaged by political conflicts between the creators and artists on the one hand (nearly all of them on the Left) and the authorities." (30) Théâtre du Soleil founder Ariane Mnouchkine,

today one of France's foremost directors, told Ardagh, "We use drama as a tool with which to fight bourgeois society." (31)
     The increasingly militant attitude of the cultural community regarding what the conservatives viewed as well-intentioned policies was of no solace to France's Communists who, by all rights, could have claimed to be the heirs to Gramsci in the same way the Italian Communists have for decades. However, although the PCF was trying to dispel its Stalinist image, few in the party leadership were willing to embrace the concept of dissent, open debate, and "the right to be different" that characterized intellectual demands in the late 1960s and 1970s.
     Gramsci's philosophy accorded better with the politics of action culturelle that developed in Socialist municipalities during the 1970s. According to Clément, the difference between the PS and the PCF was that while both supported increased aid for artistic creation, only the Socialists were interested in giving culture a participatory dimension through education and group animation. (32) The Socialists were reacting to the "conformity" of modern culture in the West, but they equally were cognizant of the dangers of totalitarianism. Policy statements by the PS continually emphasized (and still do) the need for government to promote individual expression and the "expansion" of the individual. Gramsci wrote that in order to combat conformism, there should be an "organizzazione di cultura" linked to the party or union, but he maintained that "the conquest of proletarian hegemony" need not mean a denunciation of free discussion or unbiased rational research. (33)
     The PS and Gramsci also shared a distrust of large-scale capitalism and its negative effects on cultural variation. (34) Mitterrand wrote in 1974, "It is worthless to expect a cultural development that corresponds to the wishes of the men and women of our country from a society dominated by the search for maximum profit." (35) In a 1977 study of the "political economy of music," Jacques Attali, now a leading economic adviser to the president, stated, "No market economy develops without reducing differences. . . . This book is not a pluridisciplinary essay, but a call for theoretical disorder." (36) Although providing a strong denunciation of capitalism, Attali's remarks also contain a stinging critique of totalitarian organization, which equally reduces differences.

FROM IDEAS TO POLICY: CULTURE AND THE NEW SOCIALIST PARTY

In their fight against hegemony during the 1960s and 1970s, the Socialists thus found themselves, as they so often have, wedged between communism and capitalism. This was, however, an excellent position from which to attract a growing and important segment of French society: the intellectuals--university teachers, scientists, engineers, administrators, members of the liberal professions, and even the graduates of the prestigious grandes écoles. According to Bernard Brown, "The increased importance of the intellectual class, given the specific characteristics of French political culture, has produced a more hostile attitude toward both capitalism and communism." (37)

As the PS searched for political legitimacy, culture was a logical area from which to appeal to the post-1968 disenfranchised intellectuals. Central to this campaign were the energy and ideas of Lang, Mitterrand's cultural adviser and the man who would become minister of culture after the Socialist victory in 1981. As a young law professor in Nancy in the early 1960s, Lang founded an international student drama festival that put the town on the cultural map. The success of the annual festival, which attracted a number of well-known Leftist theater groups as well as fringe directors, confounded conservative authorities locally and in Paris, and some in Nancy even accused Lang of having "prepared May 1968" by bringing together so many youths "with long hair, strange clothes, and scandalous behavior." (38) Lang's notoriety, however, eventually won him an appointment as director of the Théâtre de Chaillot in Paris in 1972. President Georges Pompidou's minister of culture, Jacques Duhamel, was reputed to be looking for a modern director to make the newly renovated Chaillot another Beaubourg. In a political power play, Giscard's first minister of culture, Michel Guy, fired Lang. The one-time lawyer and former Parti Socialiste Unifié (PSU) member then offered his services to the growing PS.

Perhaps more than anything else, Lang and his ideas came to embody the meaning of action culturelle. As a dynamic provincial cultural animator and later frustrated national cultural leader, he represented a sense of hope and promise for a new beginning that many believed only the Socialists could provide for French culture. Lang was "a utopian of the possible," lauded the Nouvel Observateur. (39)

When questioned, Lang maintains that he never developed a general theory of culture but rather borrowed from the ideas of the Popular Front, Malraux, and the philosophers of 1968. He claims that his own philosophy can be summarized in one short question: "How can one liberate creative initiative?" It is clear that he believes he came closest to finding the answer while running the festival at Nancy. "I called on the people to take part," says Lang. "Nancy started out as avant-garde but became a popular festival because the people got involved." (40)

Lang's belief in what he accomplished in Nancy formed the basis for Eclats, a book, actually a series of dialogues, he co-wrote with his friend, author Jean-Denis Bredin. The introduction, in which Bredin idolizes Lang as the champion of the "new" French culture brutally silenced by Giscard, reveals the easy acceptance of Gramscian ideas into the Socialist mainstream in the 1970s. According to Bredin's critique of the state of French culture in the Giscard era, the "Parisian bourgeoisie," which controlled the country's economic and political life, had reduced its interest in culture to an empty concept of classical knowledge, appropriate for passing an administrative concours or making polite dinner conversation. The "ruling class" had removed all imagination from contemporary culture, leaving it a uniform, mass market preserve. The final defiant message: "In the cultural desert that covers France, the pioneers of an innovative action culturelle are at work." (41)

THEORETICAL DILEMMAS AND THE COUNTERCULTURE

Although countercultures emerged throughout the West at the end of the 1960s, in no country but France did they achieve such important recognition by a leading political party. While perhaps a measure of the polarization of society in the 1970s or just a continuation of the twentieth-century cycle of culture, politics, and crisis, the Socialist decision to adopt what in other countries was treated as an intellectual fringe raised long-term questions for the future of politics and the arts in France. First among these questions was whether France's "new" cultural leaders could bring about real change in the debate between proponents of elitist versus popular culture. The Communists, although casting themselves as France's chief "alternative" since World War II, largely had failed to articulate a new vision of culture beyond the interests of its own Parisian intelligentsia. However, while Lang and his supporters were unanimous in their condemnation of a Parisian bias in cultural spending and decision-making, it remained to be seen whether <u>action culturelle</u> would not create a new elite, as unresponsive to public interest as what existed previously. A secondary question surrounding the Socialist cultural project was how well it would survive France's well-known bureaucratic phenomenon. The counterculture attacked Malraux and his successors for institutionalizing culture to the point that it strangled creativity. Similarly, the Communist approach was rejected as providing structure without soul. As the fresh ideas of 1968 were incorporated into the Socialist mainstream, however, they would have to undergo some sort of transformation if they were to be put into effect, first at the local level and then as part of a national cultural policy. As many artists later realized, embedded in the Socialist program was a commitment to build perhaps the free world's largest cultural bureaucracy.

The final consideration was what kind of political objectives the Socialists realistically could hope to achieve. While socialist tradition and newfound Gramscian ideology saw culture as a useful element in the peaceful transformation of society, the explosive world of contradiction promised by the counterculture held no promise that artists and intellectuals would move society in any single direction once barriers to cultural expression were removed. It would appear that the the Socialists were taking a gamble; their interest was to allow for a clash of ideas that might stimulate people to think in new ways, to encourage a debate out of which a new definition of culture and society could emerge. This vision has consistently been articulated by Lang. In his doctoral dissertation, "The State and the Theater," he wrote, "Culture is more a result than an ingredient. A soft and docile culture corresponds to an aged society; a combative and independent culture belongs to a living one." (42) When asked by an American journalist whether culture was part of politics, Lang responded, "Yes. In the importance of a spirit. . . that can change society." (43)

President Mitterrand, it seems, shared his minister's notion of culture. "But perhaps good plays, books, movies, or paintings are not what the Socialists are after at all," wrote E. J. Dionne, Jr., in evaluating the Sorbonne Conference. "Mr. Mitterrand argued in effect that the twists and turns of Socialist cultural policy might be explained by the search for something new. And what he was seeking sounded as much like a new political philosophy as anything else." (44)

NOTES

1. George A. Codding, Jr., and William Safran, Ideology and Politics: The Socialist Party of France (Boulder, Colo.: Westview Press, 1979), p. 39.

2. Jean Jaurès, "Pour la Laique," in L'Esprit du Socialisme, Jean-Louis Ferrier, ed. (Paris: Editions Gouthier, 1964), p. 174.

3. Francois Mitterrand, "Un Choix Culturel," L'Unité, May 10-16, 1974.

4. Pierre Gaudibert, Action Culturelle: Intégration et/ou Subversion (Paris: Casterman, 1971), p. 9.

5. As quoted in Charles S. Maier, Recasting Bourgeois Europe (Princeton: Princeton University Press, 1981), p. 32.

6. "Création et Consommation Musicales: Le Grand Ecart," Esprit, March 1984, p. 61.

7. Claude Petit-Castelli, La Culture à la Une (Paris: Club Socialiste du Livre, 1981), p. 28.

8. Paul Puaux, Les Etablissements Culturels (Paris: La Documentation Francaise, 1982), p. 12.

9. Jean Jaurès, L'idéalisme dans la Conception de l'Histoire, 1894. As quoted in Etienne Gout et al., "La Politique Sociale du Front Populaire" in Léon Blum, Chef du Gouvernement, 1936-1937 (Paris: Librairie Armand Colin, 1967), p. 275.

10. Evelyne Ritaine, Les Stratèges de la Culture (Paris: Presses de la Fondation Nationale des Sciences Politiques, 1983), p. 21.

11. Codding, p. 37.

12. Gout, p. 270.

13. Gilbert Ziebura, Léon Blum et le Parti Socialiste, 1872-1934, Jean Duplex, trans. (Paris: Librairie Armand Colin, 1967), p. 104.

14.   Léon Blum, introduction to 2d edition of Du Mariage
(1937), as quoted in James Joll, Three Intellectuals in Politics
(New York: Harper & Row, 1960), pp. 23-24.

15.   Pierre Cabanne, Le Pouvoir Culturel Sous la Ve
République (Paris: Olivier Orban, 1981), p. 18.

16.   Leo Lagrange, numéro special de Vu, July 25, 1936, as
quoted in Gaudibert, p. 31.

17.   Nowhere was the cultural clash between the Popular Front
and its totalitarian neighbors more evident than at the 1937
Paris World's Fair.   For more details, see Thomas G. August,
"Paris 1937:   The Apotheosis of the Popular Front," Contemporary
French Civilization, vol. V, no. 1, Fall 1980.

18.   Cabanne, p. 142.

19.   Ibid., p. 58.

20.   Marc Fumaroli, "De Malraux à Lang: l'excroissance des
Affaires Culturelles," Commentaires, Autumn 1982, p. 247.

21.   Gaudibert, p. 42; Cabanne, p. 140.

22.   "André Malraux S'Explique. . ." Le Nouvel
Observateur, October 14, 1968, p. 7.

23.   Francois Mitterrand, Ici et Maintenant (Paris: Librairie
Arthème Fayard, 1980, p. 159.

24.   As quoted in Cabanne, p. 141.   Louis Althusser first
borrowed from Gramsci when he introduced the concept of
"appareils idéologiques" in various institutions that determine a
society's culture in his 1965 book Pour Marx. See Gaudibert, pp.
51-52.

25.   Catherine Clément, Rêver Chacun Pour l'Autre (Paris:
Librairie Arthème Fayard, 1982), p. 85.

26.   Jacques Texier, "Gramsci in Francia," in Gramsci e la
Cultura Contemporanea II (Rome: Editori Riuniti--Istituto
Gramsci, 1970), p. 379.

27.   Gramsci, The Prison Notebooks, as quoted in Leonardo
Salamini, The Sociology of Political Praxis (London: Routledge &
Kegan Paul, 1981), pp. 59, 127.

28.   Salamini, p. 18.

29.   Jean-Marc Piotte, La Pensée Politique de Gramsci (Paris:
Editions Anthropos, 1970), p. 214.

30.   John Ardagh, The New France: A Society in Transition

(Harmondsworth, Middlesex, England: Penguin Books, 1973), p. 607.

31.   Ibid., p. 604.

32.   Clément, p. 79.

33.   Paolo Bonetti, _Gramsci_ _e_ _la_ _Società_ _Liberaldemocratica_ (Rome: Laterza, 1982), pp. 115-116.

34.   Bonetti notes that Gramsci was an admirer of American antitrust laws for just this reason (p. 118).

35.   Francois Mitterrand, "Un Choix Culturel."

36.   Jacques Attali, _Bruits_ (Paris: Presses Universitaires de France, 1977), p. 11.

37.   Bernard E. Brown, _Socialism_ _of_ _a_ _Different_ _Kind:_ _Reshaping_ _the_ _Left_ _in_ _France_ (Westport, Conn.: Greenwood Press, 1982), p. 185.

38.   Jack Lang and Jean-Denis Bredin, _Eclats_ (Paris: Jean-Claude Simoen, 1978), p. 13.

39.   Guy Dumur, "Un utopiste du possible," _Le_ _Nouvel_ _Observateur_, March 4, 1978, p. 79.

40.   Jack Lang, personal interview with author, Paris, July 15, 1986.

41.   Jean-Denis Bredin, preface to _Eclats_, p. 22.

42.   Jack Lang, _L'Etat_ _et_ _le_ _Théâtre_ (Paris: Librairie Générale de Droit et de Jurisprudence, 1968), p. 344.

43.   Jack Lang, "L'Heure de Vérité," Antenne 2 TV, September 12, 1982.

44.   E. J. Dionne, Jr., "Culture Meeting in Paris Sets Off Debates," _New_ _York_ _Times_, February 21, 1983, p. C9.

2
The Road to 1981:
Local Roots of
a National Policy

Changer la Vie;
On Va Vivre Mieux, Parce qu'on Va Vivre Autrement*

<u>PS</u> <u>Campaign</u> <u>Slogans</u>

A distinct cultural appeal was implicit in Socialist party campaigns throughout the 1970s. In addition to the ideological factor, the emphasis on culture also made good political sense. Writing in 1975, Jacques Rigaud, <u>directeur</u> <u>du</u> <u>cabinet</u> during the early 1970s for Pompidou's minister of culture, Jacques Duhamel, commented, "Situated where it is on the political checkerboard, the Parti Socialiste is at a crossroads which leads to much interest in its position on culture." (1) Rigaud warned that the Left had been handed a monopoly over political reflection on culture and that the Right was wrong "not to consider the theme to be electoral." (2)

In the years following 1968, a range of new constituencies --few drawn from the "working class"--came to identify themselves with the newly formed PS, all of them with strong cultural interests. Intellectuals who were discouraged by the Communist party's failure to wholeheartedly support the May events became disillusioned and left the PCF in droves, thereby cracking what many saw as a Communist monopoly as the voice of France's intellectuals.

Professors and teachers, traditional supporters of the socialists, joined the reconstituted PS early on and in numbers that far outweighed their presence in society as a whole. More important, the PS increasingly became the effective spokesman for the growing middle class made up of executives, technicians, and social workers. All were part of a new public for the arts, a public with new tastes and a desire for greater cultural decentralization out of Paris and more local intiative in their communities. (3)

---

* Change Life; We'll live better, because we'll live differently.

Throughout the 1970s, the PS rebuilt itself as a traditional party of the workers but one in which members of the cultural constituencies mentioned above maintained a disproportionate influence. Indeed, many of the smaller factions that joined to form the PS were almost entirely composed of intellectuals and academics. Workers represented only 16 percent of the membership of the PSU in 1971, three years before its leader, Michel Rocard, joined the PS. (4) (Many of the leaders behind the Socialist cultural policy were PSU members, including Lang and Grenoble mayor Hubert Dubedout). Only one of thirty delegates at a 1973 PS national congress in Grenoble was a worker. (5) A survey of the Gironde (Bordeaux) region in 1974 found that of those socialists who were members of interest groups (62 percent of total), only half belonged to one of the three major trade unions. More than 17 percent were members of the Fédération de l'Education Nationale (FEN), the teachers' union. (6)

By the time Mitterrand was elected president in 1981, the PS already had earned the nickname "le parti des profs." In a study of the makeup of the new National Assembly (1981), journalist André Passeron found 147 teachers and professors among the 285 socialist deputies. The Communists had thirteen, Giscard's Union Des Democrats Francais (UDF) had six, as did Chirac's Rassemblement pour la République (RPR). The PS delegation also counted 13 alumni of the elite, intellectually prestigious Ecole Nationale d'Administration (ENA), three more than the combined total of both the UDF and RPR. (7)

Codding writes that "free lance intellectuals, academics, and professional politicians have continued to dominate the executive organs of the PS, and such domination has undoubtedly had an impact on the party's orientation." (8) In terms of cultural policy, this statement was as true prior to 1981 as it is today. Culture was never a priority of the labor unions or the "workers," but rather it was promoted by smaller, well-educated constituencies who exercised a disproportionate influence on the PS, first at the local level and, later, in Paris.

The purpose of this chapter is to explore the development of cultural initiatives by Socialists at the local level during the 1970s and to underline the similarities and differences--of ideas and people--between these early efforts and post-1981 Socialist cultural policy.

CULTURE IN THE SOCIALIST MUNICIPALITIES

In its bid for power during the 1970s, the PS followed a path of building local loyalty through effective municipal administration and translating that loyalty into legislative victories. By the end of the decade most of France's major cities were under Socialist or joint Socialist/Communist leadership. One aspect of the changes wrought by local Socialist officials was a heavy emphasis on cultural affairs and quality-of-life issues.

While cultural expenditures of the national government fell to an historic low of .48 percent of the total budget under Giscard, cultural spending was on the rise in major French

Table 1

Cultural Spending of Selected Socialist Cities, 1978-1981

	Culture as % of total budget, 1978	Culture as % of total budget, 1981	% growth cultural spending per capita, 1978-1981
Angoulême	11.2	12	+54
Avignon	20.3	22	+13
Belfort	8.9	14	+101
Bourges	8.5	10	+11
Brest	9.2	13	+6
Grenoble	14.3	12	+4
Montbéliard	8.5	16	+69
Montpellier	7.1	11	+64
Rennes	8.4	12	+40
Valence	7.3	10	+34

Source: Ministry of Culture. Développement Culturel, nos. 55, 59.

cities. In 1978, a Ministry of Culture study found that eighteen cities were already committing more than 10 percent of their budgets to cultural affairs (see table 1). By 1981, cultural spending had grown substantially throughout the country with many cities reporting increases of between 50 and 100 percent. (9) New Socialist mayors, in their eagerness to mark a visible change in their communities, were most closely identified with promoting a more active role for city hall in cultural life. The phenomenon was especially evident in such tourist centers as Avignon and Grenoble but was also quite strong in industrial cities such as the automobile center of Montbéliard and Lille, whose mayor, Pierre Mauroy, would later become Mitterrand's prime minister.

Taking the Initiative

By promising more credits for cultural activities and a commitment to organized cultural planning, the PS won the loyalty of many who felt that the Right had relegated their interests to a low priority. Recognition and funds were given to smaller, more flexible organizations that promoted arts festivals and "sociocultural" groups dedicated to special programs for youth and minorities (mostly North African immigrants). Nonprofit, middle-class associations, whose interests in expanding culture in the provinces coincided with those of the PS, were also important elements of the new municipal cultural policies. John Ardagh notes, "A fair share of suburbia's new pioneers are politically motivated. . . and many of their community ventures thus become politicized, including those that have nothing to do with politics, such as sport or music." (10) In some cases, such as Grenoble and Rennes, members of cultural associations were instrumental in bringing the Socialists to power.
Despite the goal of including private associations and other organizations as equal partners, the expansion of municipal cultural spending tended to strengthen the role of mayors and their staffs. As a sign of the increased importance of culture in municipal government, most mayors appointed full-time aides (_adjoints chargés des affaires culturelles_) in charge of implementing cultural policy. In the Socialist communities, aides were encouraged to take an active stance. As one _adjoint_ stated,

> We no longer wish to be simple purveyors of funds. We want to provoke encounters, to build a program that interests everybody, to bring the associations together to take an active part in the development of a town cultural project. (11)

In general, the _adjoints_ emerged as the real power brokers in terms of making key policy decisions and doling out subsidies. (12)
The PS summarized the policies of _action culturelle_ in various town halls throughout France as _La Culture à la Une_, underlining the unity of local efforts and the emphasis on common goals. In sharp contrast with the Communist municipalities,

which took an extremely rigid and traditional approach, priority
in the Socialist towns was given to the "democratization of
culture." This meant a commitment to a dialogue with artists and
existing cultural institutions, more efforts to introduce culture
at the neighborhood level, and a greater stress on teaching.
Communities were encouraged to "refuse banalization, to make
culture a deep, explosive shock of contradictions, and to refuse
standardization while constantly recognizing the 'right to be
different.'" (13)

The primary concern of the cultural policies, according to
Socialist officials, was to raise awareness and remove all
barriers to cultural institutions and creativity. This was to be
accomplished primarily through a process that became known as
"animation." While the term came to be a catchall for almost
anything, animation activities were supposed to be characterized
by spontaneity and active group learning. The concept dated back
to diverse local experiences of working and more often
middle-class associations starting after World War II, but it
acquired a stronger ideological significance during the late
1960s as ideas of community self-reliance and social change came
into fashion. The earliest PS statements on <u>action</u> <u>culturelle</u>,
such as the Chateauvallon conference (1971) and Francis Jeanson's
<u>L'Action</u> <u>Culturelle</u> <u>Dans</u> <u>la</u> <u>Cite</u>(1973), saw an expansion of
"animation" as critical to the accomplishment of the Socialist
dream of transforming society and creating a "living" culture.

While never as well organized as the Communist party--which
maintained a centralized grip over its municipalities--the
Socialists claimed to be building a common experience. "The
contrast is flagrant," wrote Grenoble Mayor Hubert Dubedout of
the differing commitments of the Giscard administration and the
Socialist municipal governments, "but the numbers cannot describe
the global coherence of these cultural policies, the fruit of an
affirmed political will." (14) At first glance, the diversity
of hundreds of different animation experiences throughout France
seems to belie any unity at all. What do a comic strip festival
in Angoulême, a sculpture project in Corbeil using rejected
pieces from a local aircraft plant, a cinema program in the rural
town of Gorron, or a play in the La Rochelle jail have in common?
There are obviously no direct links, but further analysis does
point to a sense of coherence around certain general
classifications that remain central to Socialist ideas of
cultural policy.

In what is probably the most thorough study of recent
municipal cultural policies in France, Roger Beaunez identifies
six principal objectives: assuring a culture of quality for all,
supporting artistic creation, diversifying/attracting a new
public for the arts, opening the definition of culture to include
new art forms, promoting cultural pluralism and the associations,
and making culture a vehicle for development. (15)

The Limits to <u>Action</u> <u>Culturelle</u>

Almost from the beginning, Socialist mayors and their
<u>adjoints</u> discovered that funding animation could not be their

only,   or even most important,   priority.   Recent studies   have
shown that all local governments, Left and Right, operated   under
similar   pressures   and   constraints as   their   cultural   budgets
expanded. (16)   With no obvious criteria for making choices, most
mayors favored   prestige projects and festivals in order to prove
to constituents that money was well spent. . Construction of new
cultural   facilities,   from theaters to museums to arts   centers,
was   often   part of the general campaign promises   of   aspiring
candidates   in the 1970s.   While Malraux's program to build a
Maison de la Culture in every department (with   costs   split
between   Paris and local government) stalled,   the   network   of
Centres   d'Action Culturelle (CAC),   two-thirds paid for by local
governments, boomed.
     Cities   also   rushed to establish their own   orchestras   and
sponsor   important theater or dance attractions.   As part of the
general   effort   to   expand   popular culture,   many   governments
sponsored municipal cinemas, either by building them outright or
more often by buying them from private owners.   Often, they were
motivated   by concerns for better quality.   At other times,
authorities   were faced with the loss of the only theater in an
entire community or quarter.   Once purchased, management of the
cinemas was   entrusted to a friendly association and   subsidies
provided.   The choice of films generally   was   made by the
association,   and   most   of the municipal theaters   became
specialized "ciné club" and "Art et Essai" houses,   dedicated not
only to showing "art" and "theme" programs but also   to   debates
and   special projects for schoolchildren,   immigrants,   and other
minority groups. (17)
     As _action_ _culturelle_ was expanded to include not only
functions of animation but also artistic   creation and the
construction of new cultural facilities, the cost of maintaining
a cultural policy escalated sharply.   The high operating   costs
of new institutions and arts facilities took an increasingly
large share of budgets, reducing the amount of money left for the
animation they were supposed to complement.   In their rush to
build new facilities and establish programs to fill   them,   few
cities took into account the long-term implications of the
expanded commitment to culture. Large subsidies often were
necessary to cover costs for many cultural events, either because
ticket prices were kept artificially low or because there was not
a sufficient audience. Subsidies originally   were   seen   as
temporary until new arts groups got on their feet and attracted a
public, but it soon became obvious that they would have to be
permanent if many of the municipal experiments,   even those that
were critically acclaimed, were to succeed.
     The efficacy of the subsidies is a subject of contention in
France as in other countries,   especially as concerns   theater,
dance,   and classical music, activities that traditionally appeal
to only a small percentage of the population.   Political
interests aside, observers agree that most of the cultural
subsidies benefit those at the top of society. While no detailed
analysis of who takes advantage of subsidies has ever been done
in France, a study prepared by the subscription office of the CAC
of Montbéliard, a small, working-class city (pop. 150,000) in the
center of a region dotted with Peugeot automobile factories,   is
revelatory (see table 2). (18)

Table 2

Maison des Arts et Loisirs of Montbéliard--
Profile of Subscribers by Profession, 1982-1983

Profession	% Women	% Men	% Total
Businessmen, liberal professions	1.11	1.03	2.14
Farmers	0.00	0.00	0.00
Artisans, shopkeepers	0.63	1.03	1.66
Executives, engineers	0.07	5.55	5.63
Intellectuals (professors, teachers, artists)	25.63	9.28	34.92
Technicians	2.22	7.69	9.92
Secretaries, clerks	9.20	2.93	12.14
Workers	0.55	2.77	3.33
Primary students	1.98	1.66	3.65
Secondary students	7.38	3.57	10.95
No profession (-60)	7.93	0.47	8.41
No profession (+60)	2.06	1.03	3.09
Other (includes unemployed)	2.38	1.74	4.12
TOTAL	61.20	38.80	100.00

Source: Subscription office, CAC of Montbéliard;
total number of subscribers was 1,260.

The 1982/1983 arts season in Montbéliard featured theater, music, dance, and variety performances by nearly eighty groups, ranging from traveling French productions and artists to such noted U.S. companies as Merce Cunningham, Pilobolus, and the New York Beaux Arts Trio. Ticket prices at Montbéliard were among the lowest in France; the same shows cost twice as much in neighboring Mulhouse, only thirty miles away. A CAC subscriber could purchase tickets for $4.00-$5.00 each, $2.50 for anyone under eighteen, students or young men doing their military service, senior citizens, and the unemployed. Receipts from ticket sales accounted for only 4 percent of the center's budget. The CAC director's justification for the policy was that no one should be excluded, especially workers and their families. In fact, as table 2 shows, the low ticket prices were a bargain for the middle class professors, teachers, administrators, and other white-collar workers who made up nearly two-thirds of the audience. Students accounted for most of the balance, and only 3 percent of all subscribers were workers.

To be fair, it must be added that the CAC offered a vast array of programs, some of them unique in France, specifically geared toward youth (production of a locally produced rock opera) and immigrants (a multimedia program about the differing experiences of North African women after immigration). However, the mounting costs of all activities were straining the budget, and had it not been for grants from the ministry the program would have been impossible. This, in turn, put the city in the embarrassing situation of trying to develop an innovative cultural policy but depending on aid from Paris to complete it.

Financial strains were perhaps the most outward sign of the 1970s culture boom, but equally important after a decade of unparalleled growth was the changed stature of culture itself. Where policies had been most successful, they inspired a growing sense of identity that went beyond the cultural sphere into politics. In Grenoble, for example, the Préfet (representative of the national government) encouraged a movement to lobby for a Maison de la Culture in the mid-1960s, a project opposed by the conservative mayor. Although starting as a strictly cultural initiative, the lobby quickly transformed the issue of the Maison de la Culture into a political one and successfully challenged the incumbent mayor. (19) Once elected, the new administration (largely made up of members of the PSU) turned Grenoble into a model Socialist city, the incubator for the culture/quality of life issues that Socialists championed throughout France in the 1970s.

At the same time, however, the philosophy of culture as an agent for social change was weakening just as the policies it inspired became successful. Animation still existed, but the animators had changed; the local militants who had begun the movement were replaced by "professionals" from the universities whose management skills may have been better, but whose ties to the community or specific associations were much thinner. (20) A similar development occurred in French theater as well. The postwar generation of directors who built up the regional theaters were replaced by a generation of Paris-born or educated directors, mostly from intellectual or upper-class origins (Lang being perhaps the best example). (21) The new cultural leaders remained ideologically committed, but while their predecessors had sought change in their communities, they were inspired by dreams of change on a grander scale--dreams that were frustrated by the financial limits of municipal governments. In the 1960s and 1970s, summarized one commentator, culture represented "the continuation of politics by other means," but by the 1980s, politics had become "the continuation of culture by other means." (22)

1981 AND BEYOND

The arrival of the Socialists to power served to cover up many of the contradictions emerging in the administration of municipal culture. Those cultural leaders, from directors to administrators whose ambitions were greater than work at the community level found new jobs higher up or added responsibilities as part of a decentralization of culture. More important, increased funds because of decentralization meant that financial pressures that were beginning to cause tensions in many municipalities would ease.

Lang and the PS campaigned hard in 1981 for a cultural budget equal to 1 percent of national expenditures. The first year's budget, overwhelmingly approved by the National Assembly and the opposition controlled Senate, reduced the share of the so-called "Grandes Institutions" (the Louvre, Pompidou Center, the Bastille Opera, and so on) from one-half of total funds to one-third. While the amount actually represented an increase in real terms, the symbolism was evident. (23) The interest of the ministry had shifted away from Paris and "classic" culture toward new ideas and projects. Lang told one interviewer,

> Administrative power is being redistributed, and economic power will be redistributed as well. Why not intellectual power? Theater people, musicians, professors have shown for some time that one can live, work, and create outside of Paris. (24)

There is no doubt that many of the ministry's policies after 1981 were inspired by specific municipal experiences. The importance of the sweeping changes that Lang brought to policy was not, therefore, one of originality, but rather the prestige and financing that accompanied the recognition that the experiments of the 1970s were more than just isolated developments. Angoulême's comic strip festival, already noted, was brought to national attention, and the ministry agreed to finance a permanent museum in the town. Popular music--rock, folk, jazz--already was supported directly or indirectly (through subsidized tickets or use of municipal concert halls and practice rooms) long before the Lang's director of music, Maurice Fleuret, decided to abandon the ministry's policy of only recognizing classical music. Citing the loss of more than 300 movie theaters in towns of 20,000 or fewer inhabitants since 1973, the ministry

pledged intervention to back up local efforts. Forty-five
million francs were budgeted for improving facilities and
production of additional copies of films for improved
distribution. (25)
     The ministry advanced a policy of signing "cultural
conventions" with representatives of regions or individual towns,
wherein both parties agreed to work toward a comprehensive plan
for cultural development. Long-range goals, specific projects,
and financing were discussed, all with an accent on action
culturelle. The government effort was headed by Dominique
Wallon, a former director of the Maison de la Culture in
Grenoble, who was named chief of the newly established "Direction
du Développement Culturelle." In addition to negotiating the
conventions, the Direction was charged with "launching new
actions destined to enlarge and enrich the cultural practices of
different social groups, especially the least favored (youth,
workers, suburban and rural residents, and students)." (26)
     The Développement Culturel program was of particular benefit
to those organizations already favored in municipalities under
Socialist administration--establishments dedicated to action
culturelle, associations, and cultural organizations in rural
areas. At the height of the program in 1983, the budget included
approximately 775 million francs as opposed to 115 million francs
spent on similar programs in 1981. (27) As figures 1 and 2
demonstrate, this subsidy, equivalent to approximately $100
million, went almost exclusively to programs and organizations in
Socialist municipalities.
     The real opportunity for the ministry to influence
decentralization was not in the towns and cities, however, but in
the regions. Municipal governments already had their own
priorities and political interests. Socialists and conservative
mayors alike wanted subsidies from Paris, but they resisted
interference and often were well equipped to do so. The new
regional governments, created by the 1982 decentralization laws,
proved to be a more cooperative and pliable partner. Just as
municipal leaders turned to culture in the 1970s in their bid to
carve out a greater political role for themselves, the regions in
the 1980s looked to the conventions as a way of asserting their
ill-defined powers. According to one study by the Centre de
Sociologie des Organisations, the policy goals of the ministry
and the political goals of the regions formed the basis for a
useful marriage of convenience. "In effect, even if the elected
officials were barely present in the negotiation over content [of
the Conventions], they took credit for the results." (28)
     The example of the lopsided relationship between the
ministry and regional governments points to a disturbing fact
behind the relationship between the ministry and local
government. Despite the conventions and other initiatives,
political decentralization of cultural policy remained an empty
promise between 1981 and 1986. The harsh reality behind the
ministry's relationship with local governments after 1981 was
that while at least initially more money was available for
cultural activities and events in the provinces, there was little
interest in shifting decision making out of Paris's control. The
Socialist commitment to spreading culture and cultural awareness

Communities Subsidized By Développement Culturel, 1982
--Cities Under Administration of the Left

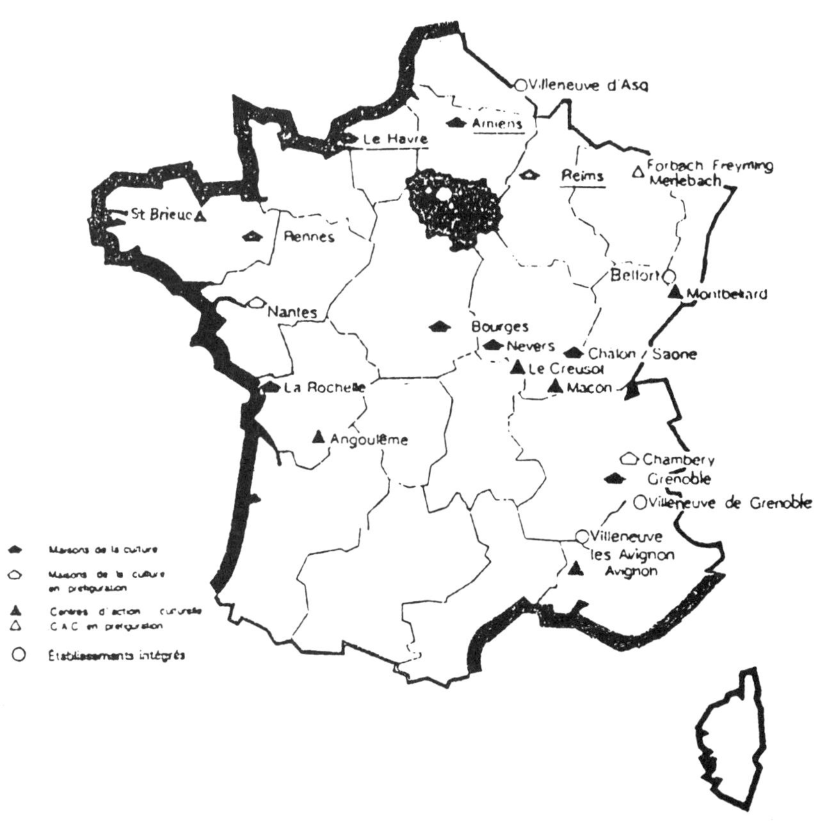

--those underlined are PCF, all others PS.

Communities Subsidized by Développement Culturel, 1982
--Cities Under Administration of the Right

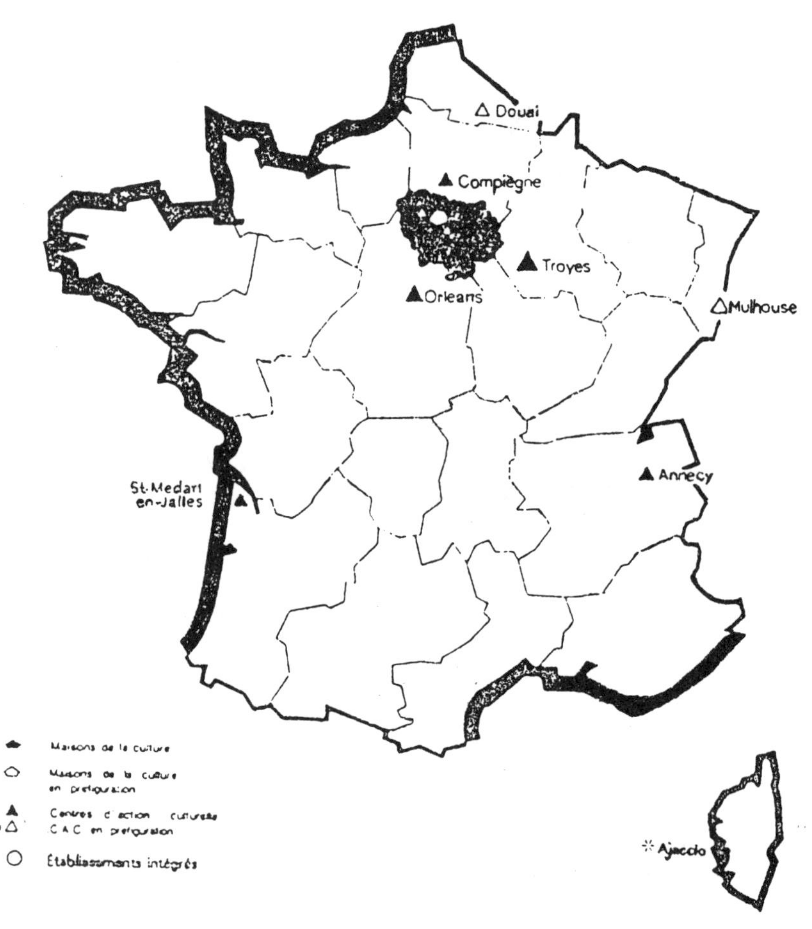

throughout the country was never in question, but it was translated into a mission of the central government; local officials, who had pioneered the whole idea of active cultural policies and _action culturelle_, were left on the sidelines while the big decisions--about decentralization and the direction of cultural policy in general--were made in Paris, where artists and administrators predominated.

NOTES

1. Jacques Rigaud, _La Culture Pour Vivre_ (Paris: Gallimard, 1975), p. 131.

2. Ibid., p. 141.

3. Michel Simonot, "Avignon 81: Un Révélateur," _Théâtre-Publique_, xi-xii, 1981, p. 58.

4. William Safran, _The French Polity_ (New York: David McKay and Co., 1977), p. 93.

5. Codding, p. 232.

6. Ibid., p. 232.

7. André Passeron, "La Nouvelle Assemblée Nationale Compte Plus de Fonctionnaires Mais Autant d'Elus Locaux que la Précédente," _Le Monde_, August 8, 1981, p. 6.

8. Codding, p. 232.

9. "Les Dépenses Culturelles des Communes," _Développement Culturel_, no. 55, April 1983.

10. John Ardagh, _France in the 1980s_ (Harmondsworth, Middlesex, England: Penguin Books, 1982), p. 316.

11. Petit-Castelli, pp. 33-34.

12. Philippe Urfalino, _L'Allocation de resources sans critères de choix: La mise en oeuvre des politiques culturelles municipales_, Doctoral thesis in sociology, 3eme cycle. Fondation Nationale des Sciences Politiques/Institut d'Etudes Politiques de Paris, 1984, p. 329.

13. Petit-Castelli, p. 163.

14. Ibid., p. 10.

15. Roger Beaunez, _Politiques Culturelles et Municipalités_ (Paris: Editions Ouvrières, 1985), pp. 33-91.

16. Urfalino, p. 248

17.   Petit-Castelli, p. 41, pp. 81-90 passim. Petit-Castelli provides a description of how three different communities--the town of Chatenay Malabry (pop. 30,000), the city of Villeurbanne (pop. 120,000), and the Paris suburb of Bondy--each came to acquire one or more publicly owned cinemas.

18.   All information pertaining to Montbéliard was gathered during a two-day visit by the author to the CAC on July 4 and 5, 1983, as the guest of the director.

19.   Claude Gilbert, "Biaiser avec la politique: L'activité culturelle à Grenoble," Esprit, March 1984, pp. 86-91.

20.   Bernard Miège et al., L'Appareil d'Action Culturelle (Paris: Editions Universitaires, 1974), p. 96.

21.   J. M. Piemme, "L'action culturelle dans tous ses états," Théâtre-Public, no. 42, November 1981, p. 20.

22.   Guy Saez, "Politique de Style, Politique de Ville (Grenoble et Rennes devant la Culture)," Cahiers de l'Animation, no. 43, 1983, p. 85.

23.   "Culture Descends from Its Pedestal," Economist, January 9, 1982.

24.   "Un entretien avec M. Jack Lang," Le Monde, September 5, 1981.

25.   Ministère de la Culture, Service d'Information et Communication, "La Nouvelle Politique du Cinéma," Le Dossier du Mois, no. 4, March 1983, p. 10.

26.   Jean-Jack Queyranne, Les Régions et la Décentralisation Culturelle--Rapport au Ministre de la Culture (Paris: La Documentation Francaise, 1982), p. 34.

27.   Ministère de la Culture, Projet de loi de finances, 1983, p. 197.

28.   Erhard Friedberg and Philippe Urfalino, La Décentralisation culturelle: La Culture au Service des Régions (Paris: Ministère de la Culture, 1984), p. 38.

3
Political Culture
and Cultural Policy

La cérémonie d'une transmission de pouvoirs, ce n'est pas
seulement de belles images à la télévision. . . c'est aussi
l'occasion de saisir le style d'un homme et la nature d'un
régime qui commence.*

Christian Fauvet, _L'Express_, May 29, 1981

From its first moments in power, the Mitterrand administration
exhibited a will to be different, a desire to make a cultural
statement. Hours after being sworn in, the president, carrying a
single red rose, made his way to the Pantheon, resting place of
socialist heroes such as Jean Jaurès and wartime-martyr Jean
Moulin. The visit underlined Mitterrand's desire to demonstrate
continuity with the past while at the same time defining a
mission for his government. After twenty-three years out of
power, most Socialists were convinced that a new era had begun.

The symbolism of inaugural ceremonies wears off quickly,
however, and the president realized that, like Léon Blum, he had
to keep one foot "in the real." The Socialists had been elected
with a long list of projects and reforms that had to be acted
upon. A large portion of French industry was nationalized,
capital punishment abolished, the minimum wage raised, the work
week shortened to thirty-nine hours, and a broad program of
decentralization initiated.

The Ministry of Culture was awarded the task of linking both
"real" and "ideal." Every reform was "culture," Lang told the
National Assembly as he presented the ministry's newly expanded
budget for 1982. Lang added that "the frontier we crossed on May
10 separates light from darkness." (1) As seen in earlier
chapters, the PS, relying upon post-1968 cultural developments
and historical precedent, had evolved toward a Gramscian concept
of culture as an ally in the program of changing society from

---

* The ceremony of a transfer of power is not only beautiful
pictures on television. . . it is also the time to grasp the
style of a man and the nature of a new regime.

within. Mitterrand wrote in 1980 that three points lay at the
foundation of the cultural project:

> A critical understanding of the cultural state of the
> country; an ethic of life based on the material and
> spiritual expansion of each individual; and a plan for
> change capable of enveloping education, information,
> science, art, in a word all that which Marxists call
> superstructures. (2)

Once Lang took office, the previously dormant, underfunded
Ministry of Culture became highly politicized, infused with a new
sense of mission. Young cultural activists from the provinces
were elevated to new jobs in Paris. After 1981, a position at
"la Culture" became prized by graduates of the ENA, a sign that
the most elite and ambitious of civil servants were reappraising
their view of the ministry, long dismissed as an administrative
backwater. Many top civil servants in other sectors of
government also applied for transfers. The ministry gained or
recuperated a number of cultural services, including the
Bibliothèque Nationale and the jurisdiction over historic
monuments and their surroundings. Lang made it clear that he did
not wish to be seen as a source of handouts or as a simple cash
register. "A policy is not just the sum of technical measures,
but first of all, it is an idea of man," he said. "I want the
ministry to expand, to abuse its own prestige. It should
contaminate the state, and the entire nation." (3) An editorial
in Le Monde, written only days after Lang took office, captured
the sense of change.

> The ministry is finally thinking about having a philosophy,
> of creating an état d'esprit. This lies at the core of the
> interviews given by Jack Lang: to know how to redefine the
> articulation of action culturelle/creation, to know on whom
> the administration can count, to know where the artists are,
> and their relationship with the public and society. (4)

The reality of government never matches political dreams.
As the Socialists discovered, it was easier to hold strong
positions on issues while in opposition than once in power. This
was as true for culture as it was for the economy, where a
program of "humane" austerity replaced dreams of state-led
expansion, or for foreign policy, where the "new" French role
in the world diverged from traditional Gaullist concepts only
with regard to relations with the USSR, which became more
restrained. Culture was only unique, perhaps, because nearly
everybody from Left to Right was convinced that a change would
and should occur. Before 1981, intellectuals and artists had
given up all hope in government and saw the Socialists as the
great promise. At the same time, Lang's initial appeal for extra
funding and support, cloaked in the mantle of Malraux and
traditional French nationalism, was welcomed by much of the
opposition as well. As Sen. Michel Miroudot, writing for the
Senate Cultural Commission, noted, "The ministry now has the
means to reanimate the ensemble of a sector that absurd economies

of an entire decade have progressively asphyxiated." (5)   The
great confidence that the Socialists would restore culture to its
proper place in French society thus held out the potential for
disillusion once the specter of competing claims, contradictory
definitions, and clashing ideas set in.

The Socialist "cultural project" lasted nearly five years,
from May 1981 to March 1986, when a Center-Right coalition
captured a majority in elections for the National Assembly.
During that time, Lang and his associates were able to proceed
with a huge number of interesting programs and policies. As a
general rule, the five years can be separated into two periods.
The first, from May 1981 through the end of 1983, was a period of
experimentation and expansion (see table 3). Money flowed easily
into nontraditional areas, and management of programs was all too
often sloppy, due to the rapidity of change and lack of
qualified, experienced personnel. As one member of a team sent
from the Ministry of Finance to the Ministry of Culture to help
supervise new budget and control procedures in 1984 put it,
"These people were poets, not administrators." The fact that a
lot of money was wasted in the early years is rarely disputed.
It is, however, a tribute to the dedication of most ministry
administrators that no major scandal in cultural spending ever
emerged despite the strong potential for it.

The second period of Lang's tenure, from 1984 through March
1986, was characterized by better organization, a sense of
urgency that time might be running out and a limited retrenchment
brought about by growing financial pressures. Many have accused
Lang of turning his attentions and those of the ministry almost
exclusively toward the 1986 elections. Lang always put a high
priority on public relations, but during his last months in
office an inordinate amount of money and energy was spent on
promotion, from glossy brochures to press conferences that took
place daily and sometimes twice in one day. When Francois
Leotard took office as the new minister of culture and
communication in March 1986, he found that the entire year's
allotment for promotional expenses already was exhausted.

The fear that the Right would win the 1986 elections had a
profound effect on spending priorities during the final two years
of Lang's tenure. The Socialists were less preoccupied with
shaping a future culture and more concerned with assuring their
place in history. Completion of the president's _grands_ _projets_
in Paris became the top priority, resulting in a return to
spending patterns favoring Paris over the provinces. In the face
of austerity, the famous "one percent" for culture survived only
because the huge outlays for some of Mitterrand's pet building
projects in the capital (the Louvre renovation, the Orsay Museum
and the Bastille Opera) were attributed to the ministry. In
perhaps the greatest irony of the Socialist cultural project,
most of the ministry's directions saw their budgets for creation,
research, and decentralization either frozen or cut after 1983.

It would be impossible to provide a meaningful summary of
every action taken by the Ministry of Culture since May 1981.
That is not, in any case, the intention of this chapter.
Instead, this chapter will concentrate on a number of the most
important themes that wove their way through much of Lang's

Table 3

Growth of Budget Outlays, 1981-1983
(FF thousands)

	1981	1982	1983
National Archives	73,181	129,756	137,229
Libraries	184,182	753,014	807,419
Book industry	13,343	53,322	60,318
Archeology	17,409	27,940	28,103
Inventory	3,914	5,121	7,213
Historic monuments	596,274	925,594	938,130
Ethnology	3,169	6,310	10,110
National museums	343,472	530,794	584,539
Other museums	39,852	121,720	92,220
Plastic arts, instruction	100,179	197,851	201,811
Artistic creation	8,326	83,058	150,880
Conservation/ restoration	50,391	98,592	107,044
Theater, creation and diffusion	276,842	537,872	616,375
Theater, instruction	7,293	13,277	13,485
Music, creation and diffusion	390,411	622,147	915,549
Music, creation and research	2,152	4,224	4,127
Music, instruction	168,214	247,764	288.341
Cinema/audiovisual	31,273	109,532	249,726
International	212	7,312	21,312
Decentralization	115,605	668,700	775,257
Studies and research	1,027	7,857	8,889
Pompidou Center	182,801	272,379	280,035
Administration	277,243	447,442	554,606
TOTAL (including other charges)	2,977,325	5,994,140	6,989,987

Source: Ministry of Culture, Le Dossier du Mois, no. 3, November 1982.

cultural policies. Examples from new and traditional areas--
theater, museums, music, plastic arts, books, and corporate
patronage--are cited to introduce various facets of the
relationship created between the Socialists, artists and the
public. Do they relate to traditional French socialist and
Gramscian concepts? Did they undermine local authority or
bolster it? In what way, if any, did they contribute to the
legitimation process? Two subsequent chapters ask the same
questions for the allied areas of broadcasting and architecture.
The primary concern throughout is with the politics of policy and
the roles played by ideological and practical concerns therein.

ART, ARTISTS, AND THE STAGE: THE POLITICS OF CREATION

The Socialists consistently used culture as a symbolic way of
presenting their entire program to the nation and the rest of the
world. Not surprisingly, the leadership took to symbolic
gestures in promoting culture itself. The campaign began shortly
after Mitterrand took office. First stop was Avignon, site of
the world-famous theater festival and annual gathering place of
the French artistic community. In short, Avignon was the perfect
opportunity for France's new political leaders to link up with
the cultural constituencies that had helped put them in power.
Mitterrand, Lang, and a host of other ministers descended upon
Avignon in force, hoping to discover a receptive audience.

Table 4

Avignon: Profile of Audience at Festival
(Figures in Percentages)

	1967	1981
20-29 years	47	28
30-39 years	17	28
40-49 years	10	15
Students	36	18
Professors/Teachers	23	32

Source: Ministry of Culture. Développement Culturel, no. 51.

In many ways, conditions could not have been better for the Socialists. The public was clearly representative of the <u>intellectuels</u> <u>de</u> <u>gauche</u>, the new intellectual class--the veterans of 1968 who had flocked to the PS throughout the 1970s. As table 4 shows, the evolution of the Avignon audience between 1967 and 1981 parallels closely the participation of the post-1968 generation in the growth of the PS (discussed in chapter 3). (6) The data suggest that the youths of 1967 were returning. Sixty percent of those surveyed in 1981 said they had already been to the festival in previous years. The maturation of the repeat audience (in terms of age and politics) is further confirmed by the declining number of students versus the increased number of teachers.

Strong ties to the PS also were demonstrated by the artists themselves. In addition to its purely cultural aspects, the festival always retains some political elements. Much to the Socialists' satisfaction, a three-day conference sponsored by the <u>Fédération</u> <u>des</u> <u>Elus</u> <u>Socialistes</u> <u>et</u> <u>Républicaines</u> attracted a great deal more interest than rival Communist meetings held at the same time, thus confirming the PS's dominant position in the cultural community. (7)

However, the picture of a solid cultural alliance of politicians, artists, and the public that appeared to emerge from Avignon was deceiving. Contrary to what might have been expected after a decade of cooperation, the PS and its cultural constituencies had much that divided them once the election victory and the "1 percent for culture" had been legislated. Many of the Socialist ideas on culture were the thoughts of artists, not administrators. Once behind a desk, painters and play directors had different values and goals than when they were active creators; the views of ministry technocrats were often even farther afield. This paradox evidently spawned discord and resentment.

Even before the Avignon festival was over, signs of ideological misunderstanding were present. Artists had looked to the PS for years as a source of support for increased financial aid and decreased interference in their daily work. For the French theater community, "decentralization" meant a freer cultural atmosphere, with responsibility shifted from the bureaucrat in Paris to the artist himself. Lang stated in his own dissertation, "The State and the Theater," any system short of total independence would result in the "creator" being squeezed between uniform state subsidies and the provincialism of local officials. However, the Ministry of Interior's decentralization program, emphasizing regional administration, only seemed to remove power from the capital and place it in the even more arbitrary hands of local governments. Michel Simonot, discussing the outcome of the Socialist cultural meetings in Avignon, summarized the conflict as follows:

> The artist was face to face with the politicians of the Left. But harmony did not reign. Especially in the theater commission, the exchanges were dominated by the artists' distrust of local officials who, under the program of decentralization, will have still broader powers over

finances and recognition. (8)

The concerns expressed at Avignon were echoed a month later by Roger Planchon, director of the Théâtre National Populaire (TNP) in Villeurbanne and the leading figure in French regional theater. An active PS supporter during the 1981 campaign, he told Le Monde that he was "disturbed" by the decentralization projects because they gave too much power to local officials. Planchon, who by the summer of 1983 refused to speak about politics at all, added, "I wish that the term 'culture' would be definitively abandoned. One no longer knows what it means. We have to return to simple terms, like 'art' and 'artist.'" (9)

Planchon's remarks underlined a general dilemma faced by the Socialists in shaping cultural policy. While in opposition, the PS was often all things to all people. A variety of local experiences could be chosen from in order to paint an image of the party as defender of high culture, popular culture, regional cultures, or immigrant cultures. Similarly, the party was at once a bastion of France's elite intellectual and artistic establishments, as well as some of the country's most important cultural iconoclasts. For some Socialists, culture was part of politics; for others culture was above it. "Art" and "artist" remained essential parts of the Socialist commitment to culture; but behind the impressive growth in the budget for arts institutions and productions of all types lay a new set of priorities that not all could be comfortable with at once.

Regionalization was opposed in the theater world because it added a series of unknown factors--namely, the presence of local officials and the public they claimed to represent--that threatened to destroy an albeit cumbersome status quo. "No one in theatrical life supports regionalization," said Michel Bataillon, Planchon's managing director at the TNP in Villeurbanne. "We're happy to rely on any minister over local authorities." (10) In practice, Lang and his deputy for theater, Robert Abirached, a much respected former director, followed their own professional sentiments and did little to actually implement the decentralization called for by PS municipal leaders. Abirached instead moved to provide a system of greater accountability for subsidized troops, requiring them to earn at least a quarter of their income through ticket sales. While this policy put many actors' and directors' worst fears to rest, it demonstrated clearly that the ministry's vision of culture was not as a free ride for artists. Creation would be supported, the public would have a limited role in the process, but the decision-making power would rest with the ministry. In the end, Abirached's ability to support innovation and growth while balancing criteria of creation enabled him to defuse the aura of political controversy that so often surrounded theater in France. He was even reappointed by Lang's conservative successor, Leotard.

Moving from theater to more general policy, "creation" and the associated concept of "research" were the two areas most often advanced by the ministry beyond the broad word "culture." There is no denying that much of the money earmarked for these areas benefited professionals in the form of study grants, refurbished studios, and government commissions. However, while creation and research were not exclusive, they were used to promote policies that often left the artists or art itself as a sideshow of a larger theme.

The debate surrounding policy changes at the Pompidou Center's Museum of Modern Art illustrated the political side of creation. The new president, Jean Maheu, wrote that a primary goal of the center was to resituate itself in the "new cultural, intellectual, and social environment that results from the evolution of techniques and from the intensive cultural policy of the government." (11) According to Pierre Schneider of L'Express, Maheu's cultural policy was little more than propaganda that substituted "speeches about art" for the "speech of art." Schneider was particularly concerned about two exhibits on art in the Third World that he believed reflected the government's political, rather than artistic, preoccupations. "Once the institution imposes its own ideas upon creation, instead of being guided by it, art runs the risk of being mutilated, censured, denatured, and devitalized," he wrote. (12)

Similar sentiments cropped up in the debate surrounding the new Orsay Museum of late nineteenth- and early twentieth-century art, a project begun by Giscard and adopted by Mitterrand as part of his grands projets. Giscard had hoped the Orsay's collection would start with Delacroix's 1830 painting Liberty Guiding the People, a hallmark of romanticism; Mitterrand chose 1848, a date closely identified with realism in art and revolution in Europe. The change in dates caused few problems until Mitterrand appointed Marxist historian Madeleine Rebérioux as vice president of the public authority charged with construction and planning of the museum. Rebérioux announced that she wished the Orsay, long planned as a bridge between the collections of the Louvre and Pompidou Center, to focus on social history and industrialization. (13) The finished Orsay Museum holds to its original mission, but Reberioux's proposal and the outcry it raised tested the limits of the attempt to situate art in a more political context.

ADMINISTRATION GUIDED BY CREATION

Had ideology been its only component, the cultural project never would have survived for five years. The Socialist objective of giving culture a role in shaping the nation's political awareness, captured in the museum debate, was a subject that quickly pitted party militants against other PS members, let alone artists, the public, and the Right-wing opposition. What gave life and broad support to Lang's ministry was not the rhetoric, which predicted a natural "mutation" of culture toward Socialist objectives, but the hands-off policies it generated, emphasizing freedom of expression and creation.

Music Policy: A Case Study of Success

Perhaps the most successful area of cultural planning during the 1980s was music, a model of the Socialist concept of "administration guided by creation." Maurice Fleuret, a former critic for the Socialist weekly <u>Nouvel Observateur</u>, took over the post of director of music with <u>little</u> administrative experience and a strong belief in the need to support creation and research. The expanded music policy came at a time when, according to <u>L'Express</u>, "after two centuries of dislike the French have begun again to adore music." (14)   While Fleuret does not take credit for the renaissance, he is clearly delighted by it.   Citing an inventory of 40,000 rock groups; 200,000 singers; and 460,000 folk-music groups, he boasts that France changed from being a country of music to a country of musicians. Policymaking, he says, involved realizing the dimensions of the change. (15)

Funding increased dramatically for most of the Direction's subsidiaries after 1981.   Fleuret's successful introduction of new priorities--previously ignored sectors (folk, rock, jazz) and the amateur practice of music--caused some grumbling from those who felt that these areas did not need special attention. However, the move was essential to demonstrate the Socialist commitment to opening up culture to the people.   According to <u>Le Quotidien</u> <u>de</u> <u>Paris</u>, "This is one way, among others, to reach a public (and voters!) whose youth is often a synonym for dynamism." (16)

No matter what sector, policy was guided by three principles: education, creation, and research (<u>formation,</u> <u>création</u>, and <u>innovation</u>).   As part of the first objective, fifty new national music schools were built.   Fleuret was frustrated, however, in his attempts to promote music education in primary and secondary schools, the only way to ensure growth in the field.   The Ministry of Education accorded music a low priority, and, worse, the lack of qualified teachers made the possibility for rapid progress a pipe dream.   As of January 1982, there were 4,000 unfilled positions for music teachers; one of every two music courses was taught by professors of French or history. (17)

Faced with almost insurmountable obstacles to promoting music through the schools, the Direction turned its attention to alternative methods of encouraging the amateur practice of music.   By far the most successful, and least conventional, idea developed by Fleuret was the Fête de la Musique, an annual event held each July that has become a global tradition.   As part of the fête, anybody who knows how to play an instrument is encouraged to come out in the streets and make music (thus creating a play on words with "<u>faites</u> <u>de</u> <u>la</u> <u>musique</u>," literally "make music").   "The Fête de la Musique is a symbolic act to demonstrate to the French the importance of music in their lives, to show them that music counts," said Fleuret in 1983, noting that Mitterrand told Lang that it was the most important thing the ministry had ever done. (18)   The success of the fête depends on the involvement of individuals playing whatever music they wish, a concept of culture that goes back to the philosophy of the Popular Front.   Although professional orchestras and music

Table 5

<u>Budget</u> <u>for</u> <u>Creation</u> <u>and</u> <u>Research,</u> <u>Direction</u> <u>of</u> <u>Music</u>

	1980	1983
Commissions	843,500	1,584,000
Research grants	390,000	1,073,000
Musical theater (includes opera)	2,000,000	10,940,000
Musical creation (prizes, new festivals)	590,000	4,842,000
Research centers	2,653,000	20,371,350
Contemporary music en-sembles	2,950,760	6,767,000
Ensemble Permanent de de Musique Contemporaine	7,564,250	10,209,800
Established festivals (La Rochelle, Metz, Or-léans, and five others)	1,515,000	3,070,000
Jazz/Variety	0	1,997,050
TOTAL	18,506,510	60,853,900

<u>Source</u>: Ministry of Culture. Direction of Music.

recitals are part of the evening's festivities, neither is the
main event. The idea promises to be around for a long time:
Minister of Culture Leotard, Lang's successor, has embraced it,
as have the leaders of forty-six countries from Argentina to
Japan.

Although promotion of amateur practice was a top priority,
the development of greater opportunity for professional musicians
and promotion of contemporary composers were equally important to
Fleuret. "Cultural life lies in innovation, not reproduction,"
he maintained. (19) Table 5 demonstrates the rapid growth in
spending for creation and research. Between 1980 and 1983, the
budget for commissions, grants, research centers, and special
projects rose nearly 600 percent. By 1985, the research budget
totaled 45 million francs, of which 26 million were earmarked
for the high-tech IRCAM center. The center has been a government
favorite for its entire ten-year history, and the added support
enabled composer/director Pierre Boulez to bring IRCAM (and
France) to the cutting edge of contemporary music, a little-known
world where computers and numerical signals are just as important
as sound itself.

The strong commitment to research may have resulted,
however, in overkill. Boulez says that Fleuret's insistence that
extra support for IRCAM be tied to the creation of additional
music research centers throughout France yielded few creative
results. "He was convinced that the large institutions stop the
small ones from functioning," says Boulez of Fleuret. "But the
large institutions are absolutely essential." (20) The new
centers were encouraged to pursue independent paths, so instead
of forming a strong French research network, Boulez developed the
IRCAM's ties abroad, particularly with institutions in the United
States.

One area of music policy in which Boulez gives the
government high marks is the emphasis on music as part of
Mitterrand's grands projets in Paris. The new opera house at the
Bastille and the conservatory and music "city" at La Villette
represent, according to Boulez, essential additions to the city's
music infrastructure which had been left untouched for five
decades. The last concert hall built in Paris before the grands
projets opened in 1924. The conservatory was housed in the same
temporary structure it was assigned in 1913, even though
enrollment had increased nearly fifteen times. The commitment to
spend money and build new facilities, says Boulez, is what sets
apart the Lang/Mitterrand relationship from that of de Gaulle and
Malraux. "There comes a time when you can no longer live on your
capital," he says. (21)

Here too, however, the Socialists' ideas may have suffered
from a desire to accomplish too much too soon. The enormous cost
of the projects and their rapid timetables were cause for concern
even among project supporters. However, as fears grew that the
Bastille Opera was at the top of the list of projects that a new
government after 1986 might eliminate or scale down, the
reaction was to accelerate construction. "It was my opinion that
it would need ten years," says Fleuret of the time required to
build the new opera. "But after four years I became a militant.
We had to profit from the support of the president of the

republic, even if it posed technical and artistic problems." (22)
The Bastille Opera was never finished (and will probably be
reduced in size and scope), but the Zenith rock concert hall at
La Villette was opened in time for the March 1986 elections.

Plastic Arts: The Shock of the New

Music was one of the more publicized aspects of the
Socialist cultural policy because of the rising popularity of
music and the high visibility and diversity of Fleuret's
projects.   However, policies of <u>formation, création</u>, and
<u>innovation</u> extended to many areas well beyond the public eye and,
sometimes, beyond public comprehension as well. Often, new
fields were attached to traditional ministerial responsibilities,
such as the addition of a large program of ethnographic research
grants to the Patrimoine division, which was charged with
maintenance and restoration of historic buildings. By far the
greatest expansion in new programs and policies took place in the
area of plastic arts--painting, sculpture, graphics, artisanal
crafts, industrial design, and photography--where an entirely new
administration was established.

The Délégation des Arts Plastiques was the brainchild of its
chief, Claude Mollard. Lang had little interest or expertise in
the area, and he placed great confidence in Mollard's fanatic
dedication to contemporary art and artists. A brilliant and
enthusiastic graduate of the ENA who built up a reputation as an
effective administrator at the Pompidou Center, Mollard is often
cited as typical of the emerging cultural technocracy. For some
he is an understanding, innovative civil servant; for others he
is a technocrat overwhelmed by the art world that surrounds him.
Mollard himself remains oblivious to any criticism, firmly
convinced that his five-year tenure as head of the delegation
created a groundswell that breathed new life into French art for
years to come.

The result of Mollard's plans to give contemporary French
artists greater opportunity to learn, create, and be better
understood by society is a range of experiences both innovative
and controversial. Because of the nature of contemporary art,
there is not much room to evaluate success or failure. Time will
be the best judge.

The plastic arts represented a unique opportunity for the
cultural project because they were part of an entirely new,
uncharted area to explore and develop. There were no previous
policies to evaluate, no commitments to adhere to, and no old
bureaucracy to hold up decisions. For those who endorsed the
establishment of new structures to serve a new culture, the field
was wide open. The French penchant for acronyms abounded as the
delegation set up agencies and centers to represent diverse
interests from comic strips and cuisine to painting and
photography.

Mollard's first step was to create a central administrative
unit called the Centre National des Arts Plastiques (CNAP). In
addition to overseeing those existing institutions assigned to
the delegation (the national art schools, the Sèvres porcelain

and Aubusson tapestry workshops), the CNAP became the principal
source of credits for almost all activities linked to the plastic
arts and a model for decentralization, a concept that had not
gained   much   ground   in   other   areas.   The delegation's
decentralization efforts were mostly planned on a regional basis
and focused on a powerful directeur régional d'action culturelle
(DRAC), who served as liaison between the ministry, local
governments, and artists and "catalyst for local initiatives for
production and diffusion." (23)

Among the programs channeled through the DRAC was the
FIACRE (Fonds d'Incitation à la Création), a special fund that
provided small grants to individual artists or for specific
projects throughout France from public murals to sculptures. One
of the more typical FIACRE/DRAC ideas was the arthothèque
program, established in thirty provincial cities.   Each
collection consists of several hundred contemporary prints and
photographs and operates like a lending library. In some cases,
the arthothèque did not purchase art but invited artists and
photographers to loan examples of their work and receive a
percentage of the modest borrowers' fees.

Although based on a Swedish model which showed lending
libraries to be a successful way of introducing contemporary art
into the homes of less privileged members of society, the French
arthothèques have not produced egalitarian results thus far.
According to a report by the ministry's research service, most
users tend to be young, well-educated professionals. (24)   Even
with the best intentions, the program appears to be yet another
example of a project that benefits the classic "cultural
constituencies" in the name of less-privileged publics.   The
arthothèques may represent a success in creating an alternative
market for contemporary art/artists, but they are a failure as
institutions for cultural transformation or social change.

In addition to FIACRE projects, Mollard developed far-
reaching regional initiatives that may qualify as the most
ambitious of all the Socialist cultural policies. The FRAC
(Fonds régionaux d'Art Contemporain) provides the seed money for
a fifty-fifty cooperative acquisitions program between the
ministry and each of France's twenty-two regional councils.
Although each FRAC committee (chaired by the Paris-appointed DRAC
but consisting of politicians and artists chosen by regional
officials) operates independently, the FRAC collectively
represents half of all public expenditure for acquisition of
contemporary art, triple the budget of the national fund that
buys art for the Pompidou Center. By 1986, the FRAC collections
totaled more than 6,000 works of art of which about one-third
were paintings and the rest mostly photos and lithographs.

The FRAC is probably the purest policy application of
diverse Socialist theories. First lies a commitment to
decentralization; second a commitment to "democratization" in
the absence of a well-developed market for contemporary art in
France; third a commitment to the development of new structures
to reach new publics. As one ministry publication described the
FRAC,

Their originality rests above all on the interest of the regions. They wanted to make them a specific instrument of _action culturelle_ and the majority have kept to their original objectives: quality and professionalism of acquisition policy, diffusion and circulation of works beyond the traditional circuits of museums. (25)

Above all objectives lies a nationalist preoccupation with restoring the old greatness of France as a world cultural presence and keeping French art in France. Socialist art critics lament that too often the state failed to recognize the value of great art and let historic opportunities slip away. The official rejection of the Impressionists is only one of many examples. Pierre Cabanne noted that because of traditional beaux arts purchasing policies, the French museums owned only one Picasso in 1936. (26)

Mollard believes that the FRAC program, by generating sufficient funds for the purpose of acquiring contemporary art and splitting the responsibility between twenty-two different committees, guarantees state support for at least some of tomorrow's great artists.   In addition, frequent roving exhibitions of the FRAC collections and associated educational projects provide an important new way of introducing contemporary art to the public at large. Mollard described the more than 200 art critics, conservators, and amateur enthusiasts who are members of the FRAC committees as "a new generation that has perhaps taken power," the "excluded" who now control "the levers of command." (27) He admits that they may make mistakes but adds, "I would have liked us to have been fooled a bit in 1930 into having twenty-two FRAC buy twenty-two Matisses, twenty-two Bracques, and twenty-two Picassos because today [these works], instead of being in American museums, would be in French museums." (28)

Almost from the beginning, the FRAC was a controversial subject in the French art world. The first complaints came from supporters of France's long-neglected provincial museums, valuable institutions that were bypassed by the FRAC.   Some claimed that money should be spent first to repair local museums and restore their already extensive collections. Others who were more favorable to the idea of buying contemporary art maintained that experienced museum conservators and their staff should make the decisions rather than the FRAC committees, many of whose members have no qualifications--and sometimes little interest--in the arts. It was originally argued that because FRAC collections would be loaned for display in museums, schools, and public buildings, the program represented a flexible, low-cost approach to art acquisition that was complementary to museums.   As the size of collections mounts, however, regions will be forced to cover greater costs for transportation and storage of works; some already have built permanent "reserves" to house parts of their collections, de facto museums free of traditional professional/ administrative requirements.

Perhaps the greatest criticism of the FRAC comes in the area of the actual acquisitions. The most severe charge leveled at Mollard is that he created an artificial market for art, supporting a generation of artists who create only for the state.

The argument appears weak in that no single artist has sold more than three or four paintings to the various FRAC; Mollard estimates that public acquisitions represent only 15 percent of the market. (29)   The concern about distortions in the art market is real, however, especially in the provinces, where private collectors are few and more likely to be influenced by regional FRAC choices.   One Lyon gallery owner, a supporter of the FRAC, comments:

> It comes back to speaking about a climate. [In Germany 1965-
> 1978]. . . there were good artists but nobody knew them.
> However, they were taken into consideration by their
> neighborhoods and towns, the municipal government or private
> enterprise which helped them exhibit, get a studio, prepare
> a portfolio. (30)

The role of galleries themselves is also a matter of dispute.   Not all FRAC purchases have been made public, a factor that raises fears that a few galleries are overcharging or, worse, dumping works they cannot sell. (31)   Complicating matters is the fact that it is impossible to evaluate the future value of the growing FRAC collections.   Everyone admits that there has been some waste, but is it worth it?   While some of Mollard's opponents believe that history will show the FRAC experience to be a disaster, it is hard not to wonder if painter Hervé Di Rosa is not right when he says, "[The FRAC] buy so much stuff, it's sure that out of ten things, one or two have got to last." (32)

The first results of the Ministry of Culture's policies to aid contemporary art and artists became evident throughout France in a relatively short time.   Large, sometimes provocative sculptures and murals cropped up in and around public buildings from palaces to railroad stations.   In addition, Mollard stressed the need to follow "Lang's method" and create events in order to attract greater public attention.   While often simply public relations efforts to get out the media, Mollard's "events" sometimes generated storms of controversy. The most celebrated event, the installation of a sculpture by Daniel Buren in the courtyard of the Palais Royal in Paris, came to symbolize the public debate over the entire cultural project--and ended up costing Mollard his job.

Daniel Buren emerged during the 1980s as perhaps the most promising sculptor in France as well as a prime beneficiary of Socialist aid for the plastic arts. His award-winning design for France's pavilion at the 1986 Biennale in Venice also has given him a new international stature. Buren always will be remembered in France, however, as the artist at the center of the last great political controversy of Lang's administration.   The problem centered on his plan, commissioned by Lang and Mollard, to transform a parking lot in the courtyard of the Palais Royal into a public plaza. Buren proposed building rows of black-and-white-striped columns, each standing at different heights. Construction got underway in the last months before the March 1986 elections and raised a public outcry. The opposition quickly focused on the columns as a desecration of the national

patrimoine, and (by implication) symbolic of Socialist
mismanagement of the state in general. Cultural officials at the
Paris city hall, Jacques Chirac's fief, tried to take legal
action to block construction. In the weeks preceding the
election, the evening news broadcasts ran an almost daily
chronicle of the verbal and legal battle surrounding the columns
against a backdrop of workers busily pouring cement at the Palais
Royal. Thousands went to visit the site and leave their thoughts
about the sculpture, Buren, Lang, and Mitterrand on the barriers
erected around it. The graffiti became a lively exhibit of
political protest art. "Socialist cemetary," wrote one bitter
observer, a thought that was perhaps on the minds of both sides.
Mollard had indeed created an event, but at what cost?

The Buren columns are at once an example of the frailty and
strength of the politics of culture in Socialist France. In the
short term, they can only be seen as a liability. Whatever
goodwill the project earned among artists (who were themselves
divided over the sculpture's esthetic merits) was not enough to
counter the public rejection of the columns--a combination of
political motivations and lack of understanding by many of
contemporary art itself. In the long term, however, the columns
will remain long after the controversy. The new minister of
culture, Leotard, refused to tear them down, citing his desire
not to set a precedent for destroying works of art no matter how
objectionable they may be. The Socialists are once again
confident that the future will show that they led the way. As
Mollard told Leotard, "Creation, by nature, bothers. And then it
is adopted: Notre Dame, the Eiffel Tower, the Pompidou Center all
have become signs of our culture." (33)

PUBLIC CULTURE, PRIVATE CULTURE

The heavy emphasis on creation in the Socialist cultural project
made capitalism an early target in many areas. Cultural
industries such as publishing, recording, and broadcasting were
essential parts of modern culture but tended to operate under the
rules of the business world. The French Left had a traditionally
negative attitude toward capitalism and was particularly
suspicious when it came to culture: large companies discouraged
innovation, and competition destroyed the ability of French
artisans to make productive cultural contributions. As late as
1981, a major opinion poll found that a majority of French
(particularly "youth, the middle class, and Socialist voters")
felt that companies "did not have a good influence on the
cultural situation." (34) Lang once explained, "In a society
where profit is the measure of everything, the sense of creation
is perverted; in a society where artists are not wholly
recognized with rights separate from others, creation dies." (35)
The argument was, of course, not new. As explained in chapter 2,
Gramsci perceived a danger in concentration and capitalism when
he wrote admirably of American antitrust laws in the 1920s.
Mitterrand and others had adopted phrasing similar to Lang's
throughout the 1970s.

Once in power, the Socialists found great difficulty dealing with the economic realities of the marketplace as they related to culture. The growth of foreign (mostly American) multinationals and their influence on French and international culture remains a topic of great contention to this day. Beyond statements at international forums, such as UNESCO, Lang's own Sorbonne Conference, or the gathering of European cultural ministers in Greece (host: actress-turned-politician Melina Mercouri, a socialist who shares many views with Lang), there is little that France can do to change the international situation, except become more competitive and register a symbolic protest from time to time. Lang surprised the entire world movie industry in 1981 by snubbing an invitation to the American Film Festival in Deauville, which rivals Cannes for national attention. Ironically, in terms of cinema, France has resisted the invasion of imports from Hollywood much better than its European neighbors (see table 6).

Table 6

Imports' Role in European Cinema Markets, 1981
(Figures in Percentages)

	U.S.A.	France	Germany	Italy	U.K.
France	35.1	--	4.1	14.2	5.0
Germany	38.4	11.0	--	17.1	4.9
Italy	44.6	23.2	8.3	--	2.3
U.K.	62.9	NA	NA	NA	--

Source: UNESCO Statistical Yearbook, 1982.

Creation and the Cultural Industries

Practical and political considerations have concentrated the thrust of policy toward the "cultural industries" on the domestic market, where Lang's efforts received mixed results. Least controversial were attempts to preserve the "purity" of the French language from a perceived onslaught of English, a ploy used successfully by de Gaulle. The policy resulted in moves to ban foreign vocabulary from advertisements as well as an amusing television campaign to promote "la magie de la langue francaise." As a further extension of these policies, Lang's successor announced regulations requiring French-language subtitles on all foreign rock videos.

In many cases, however, what outsiders perceived as traditional French snobbery and chauvinism in defending their culture was part of a concerted political effort to build up new industries and jobs in France. The linkage of economy and culture was a critical element in Lang's bid to lift the status of French culture in public opinion. In a time of crisis, he believed, culture had to be seen as a source of hope. With traditional industries such as steel and autos in decline, Lang argued that France should fall back on its culture as a source of thousands of new jobs in such areas as publishing, recording, moviemaking, and musical instrument manufacture.

Although past governments set a precedent for aid to the cultural industries by establishing subsidies for publishing and film production, no program as extensive as that proposed by Lang had ever been dreamed of. Funding was established to guarantee loans and subsidize new projects in artisanal and craft industries. More controversial was the boost given to the fashion industry as a result of the ministry's sponsorship of the Musée de la Mode on the Rue de Rivoli. A concerted effort to revive French furniture design also was spearheaded by the ministry through direct grants and commissions for remodeling public buildings such as the Elysée Palace, a project which propelled designers Philippe Starck and Jean-Michel Willmotte into the public eye.

The emphasis on "economy and culture," while appearing contradictory to socialist philosophy, was essential to the success of the cultural project in the 1980s. The Socialists were interested in changing perceptions of culture from a distant, removed area to a central factor in daily life. In a country as traditional as France, equating videos, armchairs, and evening gowns with paintings and opera was all part of the move to break up the elitist psychology surrounding the word "culture" and, once again, to bring in the excluded.

However, while the ministry's commitment to building the cultural industries tended to gain support from artists and the public alike (producers and consumers, so to speak), there were some notable exceptions. As the experience of the law regulating book sales demonstrates, the marriage of economy and culture was at times explosive.

<u>Regulating the Book Industry: A Case Study</u>. During the 1981 election campaign, Mitterrand charged the Giscard government with complete disregard for culture, noting that books were treated

with as much respect as toothbrushes. (36)   Mitterrand was referring to the widespread discounting of books as practiced by large department stores and chains.   The Socialist position was that discounting overconcentrated the book market in the hands of a few large retailers to the detriment of small bookstores and publishing houses who were willing to stock and publish significant works as well as bestsellers.   Rampant capitalism, the Socialists maintained, threatened the French publishing industry and, by extension, French writers.

One of the first cultural measures approved by the new parliament in the summer of 1981 was a unitary price law for books (the so-called Loi Lang).   Under the law, which took effect on January 1, 1982, books had to be sold within a margin of 5 percent of a publishers' list price. The measure was passed with near unanimity, largely for political reasons on all sides. According to National Assembly cultural rapporteur Rodolphe Pesce (PS), the law marked a highpoint in legislative lobbying. (37) In the end, deputies and senators supported small bookstore owners in their home districts and overrode the pressure from large Paris-based retailers and big publishing houses.

Writers as well as small editorial houses and neighborhood booksellers are, needless to say, quite satisfied with the new law. The public that buys books, especially students and teachers, is furious. In addition to the end of discounts, book prices rose well ahead of the inflation rate, as table 7 demonstrates, for the first four months of 1982. Lang's support

Table 7

Book Prices after Application of Loi Lang, 1982

		Book Price Index	
Month	CPI	Scholarly	General
January	+1.03	+1.60	+1.86
February	+1.02	+2.00	+2.10
March	+1.15	+2.39	+3.26
April	+1.19	+1.10	+1.40

Source: Ministry of Culture/INSEE.

for the law, based on the need to save the diversity of the French publishing industry, remained steady despite public protest and legal challenges that went as far as the European Court of Justice. The court's refusal to invoke the European Economic Community's competition rules to strike down the book law is of special importance since it provides an important legal boost to supporters of special treatment for "cultural industries" throughout Europe.

In France, the unitary price law most seriously affected sales of the Fédération Nationale d'Achat de Cadres (FNAC), a unique chain that specializes in high-volume, discount sales of books, records, and photographic supplies. The FNAC was founded in the 1950s by two young Trotskyites as a type of cooperative store charging the lowest possible prices for the benefit of its members, who by 1980 numbered in the hundreds of thousands. The firm also has taken on a role as consumer and cultural advocate and spends 1 percent of its budget on cultural activities, a rare occurrence in a country that has little tradition of corporate arts patronage and, until recently, no tax incentives. In 1981, the chain's eleven stores controlled 9 percent of the French record market, 10 percent of the photography market, and 14 percent of all book sales. (38)

The FNAC's expansion into the book market took place primarily during the 1970s, with stores placed in Paris and major university centers offering 20 percent discounts on a wide selection of books. According to sociologist Priscilla Clark, the opening of the first FNAC bookstore in Paris "provoked cries of outrage and dark intimations that such un-French and unliterary practices portend the demise of French literature itself." (39) According to Clark, the attitude is typical of the "entrenched elite orientation of French literary culture."40 Despite its phenomenal success, the FNAC always has had enemies among those who considered literature as an art or adventure, separate from business. As the socialist-oriented _Nouvel Observateur_ explained, the competitiveness discouraged impulse buying at local bookstores where prices were higher, restricted the number of titles a store would keep on hand, and (heaven for forbid!) provided a precedent for other mass marketers such as supermarkets "to sell best-sellers, at cost, falling over the ravioli." The _Nouvel Observateur_ continued, "Disturbed by the dangers that the FNAC could cause for literary creation, Francois Mitterrand came out in support of a unitary price in 1977." (41)

While Mitterrand came to share the fears of the French literary elite, he was clearly out of step with the feelings of the FNAC's members, whose demographics reveal striking similarities with the traditional Socialist cultural constituencies identified in chapter 3. According to the Ministry of Culture, a breakdown of the FNAC's patrons in 1981 shows a highly educated group of youths aged 15 to 24, managers and alumni of the _grandes écoles_, members of the liberal professions, and students. (42)

In an open letter to Lang, an outraged _Le Monde_ reader called for a consumer strike to protest the Loi Lang and the poor treatment of the FNAC. At the same time, the letter underlined the growing estrangement between Lang and certain segments of the population that had been taken for granted:

> I am a professor of French and contemporary literature . . .
> and I write, which is to say that books are my life. Except
> for paperbacks, I never could buy books until the FNAC
> opened its bookstore. For the first time, books were sold
> at an affordable price.
> Will this be the first abominable law instituted under
> Mitterrand? I voted for him, thinking, I suppose like the
> majority, that this hasty clause in his program would be
> corrected by wisdom and consultation with readers.
> How can one promote creation and aid writers by
> diminishing the number of buyers? I will not be the only
> reader to strike ... if only in the library." (43)

As the Socialists discovered with the unitary price/FNAC case, some cultural policies, born out of a genuine commitment to the arts, may serve to weaken the party's support from its cultural constituencies. It demonstrated an inherent weakness in the party's approach to culture since clearly, in this case, the cultural community was not one. Artists had their own interests, and, in siding with them, the party was construed to be taking an elitist position. The difficulty the Socialists had in dealing with the FNAC also represented an old idea of capitalism as an adversary of culture, just at the moment when it was becoming outmoded.

Opening the Door to Corporate Culture

At the same time that Lang was taking an unwavering stand against mixing capitalism and culture in the book industry, he demonstrated unusual flexibility in reaching out toward business as a partner in supporting the arts. Mécénat, as corporate sponsorship is called, was about as new an idea to France as it was to the Socialists in the early 1980s. Much of the credit for its promotion from relative obscurity goes to Jacques Rigaud, a remarkable fixture on the French cultural scene. The numerous titles he has held since serving as deputy to Pompidou's minister of culture, Jacques Duhamel, include president of the Franco-Luxembourg television station RTL and president of the public agency charged with building the Orsay Museum. As chairman of ADMICAL (Association pour le Développement du Mécénat Industriel et Commercial), a civic group dedicated to promoting mécénat in France, Rigaud has tried to use his influence and prestige to push for fiscal incentives and, more important, to create an appropriate attitude about patronage within the business community.

Corporate patronage in France remains an anomaly, in sharp contrast to the experience of many other Western countries. The explanation for this situation is probably linked to the same factors behind the unusual strength of the French Ministry of Culture: centuries of tradition have made the state paramount, completely replacing the notion of individual patronage. Until very recently neither the business community nor the French public was ready to accept <u>mécénat</u>, as ADMICAL's mission demonstrates.

Although Lang gave verbal support to the idea of private involvement in the arts, the ministry was slow to act on any concrete plan. The huge increase in public funds available during the first few years dampened interest in the private sector as cultural officials were busy developing their own programs. Real interest in <u>mécénat</u> only developed as budgets tightened after 1984, when talk of cofinancing of initiatives suddenly emerged. Corporate leaders, however, shied away from the role of picking up the pieces of state initiatives and pressed for concessions to allow the private sector to expand its own commitments. In 1985, Lang pushed through two important fiscal reforms that could eventually pave the way for real growth of <u>mécénat</u>. The first reform doubled the ceiling for cultural deductions on taxable revenue from .1 percent to .2 percent. A separate law created tax shelters designed to promote private motion picture production. Businesses and individuals are now permitted to buy shares in private production companies known as SOFICA (sociétés de financement des industries cinématographiques et audiovisuelles) and write part of the investment off their taxes. Taken together, the measures showed for the first time that the state was serious about the private sector having a role in creation and development of culture.

By adopting the cause of <u>mécénat</u>, Lang had something to gain and nothing to lose. At a time of austerity, any new source of funds was worth cultivating. Similarly, involving corporations in the arts provided an answer to those critics who accused the ministry of trying to dominate cultural life. It also stole a potential issue from political opponents. In addition, the same 1981 poll that showed the public had a negative attitude toward companies in general revealed support for those practicing <u>mécénat</u>. (44) Even organized labor (with the exception of the Communist-dominated Confédération Générale du Travail (CGT) appeared to endorse the idea of a cultural role for enterprises. (45)

Surprisingly, the lead in corporate sponsorship of the arts in France was taken by the subsidiaries of American companies such as IBM, Singer, Kodak, and Fisher Price, all winners of ADMICAL awards in 1980 and 1981. The American efforts often represent an extension of patronage traditions established by parent companies. Participation by French firms, especially state-owned banks and companies, has grown rapidly in the past few years, however. Sponsorship choices range from individual events and projects to corporate foundations dedicated to specific areas, such as the Apple Foundation for Cinema and the Johnson Foundation for Theater. Less frequent, but well publicized, are the private art and sculpture collections of the Cartier Foundation outside of Paris and the Maeght Foundation in St. Paul de Vence near Nice.

While most corporations prefer to be identified with traditional art forms and activities that attract vast public attention such as festivals and art exhibits, a few have been more innovative. A small brick manufacturer, Heem, in northern

France won an award from ADMICAL in 1982 for sponsoring seven sculptors with space to work and unlimited supplies of bricks and cement. Renault Art Industrie, a 2-million-franc annual program sponsored by the state-owned auto company, commissions original works from contemporary artists; in 1985, the company donated car bodies to monumentalist sculptor Bill Woodrow for a work exhibited at the Paris Biennale.

Despite encouraging developments, the first comprehensive study of corporate mécénat, completed by the Ministry of Culture in 1986, revealed that mécénat remained small-scale. Author Guy de Brebisson estimated that using the most liberal of definitions, only 400 companies are involved, spending approximately 350 million francs each year. (46) The study, based largely on the responses by eighty companies to questionnaires, also found that in most cases the president of the company was directly involved in the decision to support the arts and often in its implementation as well. While none of the supporters of private sponsorship believes that it will ever supplant the state role, it remains to be seen whether the Socialists, who made culture a top priority of government, also will be credited with making it a top priority of business as well. It would not be the greatest of ironies of France's changing political culture.

NOTES

     1.   Jack Lang, speech on presentation of culture budget to the Assemblée Nationale, November 17, 1981.

     2.   Francois Mitterrand, _Ici_ _et_ _Maintenant_, p. 156.

     3.   "Un entretien avec M. Jack Lang."

     4.   Claire Dévarrieux, "Nouveau Départ," _Le_ _Monde_ _des_ _Arts_ _et_ _des_ _Spectacles_, June 11, 1981, p. 16.

     5.   Sénat. Commission des Affaires Culturelles. _Avis_. (no. 59), sur le projet de loi de finances pour 1982, adopté par l'Assemblée Nationale, Tome I, "Culture," November 23, 1981, p.7.

     6.   All statistics regarding the Avignon festival come from Ministère de la Culture, Service des Etudes et Recherches, _Développement_ _Culturel_, no. 51, March 1982.

     7.   Simonot, p. 57.

     8.   Ibid., p. 64.

     9.   Claude Régent, "Une Année de Transition pour Roger Planchon," _Le_ _Monde_, September 17, 1981.

     10.   Michel Bataillon, personal interview with author. Villeurbanne, June 24, 1983.

11.   Pierre Schneider, "Beaubourg: Chefs-d'oeuvre sous Surveillance," L'Express, .March 2, 1984, p. 8.

12.   Ibid., p. 8.

13.   Francois Chaslin, Les Paris de Francois Mitterrand (Paris: Gallimard, 1985), pp. 48-53.

14.   Evelyn Fallot, "La Folie de la Musique," L'Express, February 2, 1982, p. 56.

15.   Maurice Fleuret, personal interview with author, Paris, July 10, 1986.

16.   "Enquête: Culture Année Zéro," Le Quotidien de Paris, April 11, 1983, p. 29.

17.   Mariella Righini, "En Avant la Musique," Le Nouvel Observateur, January 2, 1982, p. 45.

18.   Maurice Fleuret, personal interview with author, 1983.

19.   Ibid.

20.   Pierre Boulez, personal interview with author, Paris, November 6, 1986.

21.   Ibid.

22.   Maurice Fleuret, personal interview with author, 1986.

23.   Délégation des Arts Plastiques, "Les Conseillers Artistiques Régionaux," undated.

24.   Natalie Heinrich, Les Arthothèques (Paris: Ministère de la Culture, 1985), p. 46.

25.   Ministère de la Culture. Service Information et Communication. La Politique Culturelle, 1981-1985: Bilan de la Legislature, "Les Arts Plastiques," p. 9.

26.   Cabanne, p. 19.

27.   Jean-Luc Chalumeau, L'art au présent. (Paris: Union Générale d'Editions, 1985), p. 75.

28.   Ibid., p. 75.

29.   "L'Etat et les Galeries d'Art," Canal, no. 56/57, Summer 1984, p. 11.

30.   Ibid., p. 11.

31.   Ibid., pp. 11-15; Chalumeau, pp. 77-78.

32. Chalumeau, pp. 77-78.

33. Claude Mollard, speech on departure from Délégation des Arts Plastiques, July 10, 1986.

34. Centre d'Information et de Diffusion Economique et Sociale (CIDES), "L'Opinion des Francais sur le Mécénat d'Entreprise," September 17, 1981.

35. Jack Lang, press conference, Lille, June 20, 1982.

36. Mitterrand, _Ici_ _et_ _Maintenant_, p. 160.

37. Rodolphe Pesce, personal interview with author, Paris, June 29, 1983.

38. Jacques Guyaz, "Innovations dans le secteur des services: du militant à l'entrepreneur," in _Francais,_ _Qui_ _Etes-vous?_ (Paris: La Documentation Francaise, 1981), pp. 195-196. Information on book sales: Ministère de la Culture. Service des Etudes et Recherches. "Les Francais et le Livre," _Développement_ _Culturel_, no. 52, October 1982, p. 4.

39. Priscilla Clark, "Literary Culture in France and the United States," _American_ _Journal_ _of_ _Sociology_, vol. 84, no. 5, March 1979, p. 1067.

40. Ibid.

41. Matthieu Lindon, "Préférez Vous Faulkner ou SAS?" _Le_ _Nouvel_ _Observateur_, August 8, 1981, p. 60.

42. "Les Francais et le Livre," p. 4.

43. Georges Grand, "Une Grève Pour la FNAC?" _Le_ _Monde_, August 7, 1981, p. 2.

44. CIDES, 1981.

45. Guy de Brebisson, _Le_ _Mécénat_ (Paris: Presses Universitaires de France, 1986), p. 110; Chalumeau, p. 151.

46. Guy de Brebisson, _Données_ _sur_ _le_ _Mécénat_ _d'Entreprise_ _en_ _France_ _en_ _1985_ (Paris: Ministère de la Culture Service des Etudes et Recherches, 1986).

4
Television

Pour ajouter à la confusion, les deputés qui s'appretent à réformer la télévision comptent parmi les Francais qui le regardent le moins.*

L'Express, April 30, 1982

It is surprising to many that television did not come under the jurisdiction of the Ministry of Culture during the Socialist years. Television, after all, has the potential to be the biggest cultural medium the world has ever known. However, in the France of the Fifth Republic, the state television monopoly also represented the largest single source of information. Any discussion of television from ownership to programming thus centered first around the news, with all other factors taking a back seat. After years in opposition, reform of the broadcasting monopoly was high enough on the Socialist agenda in 1981 to warrant the appointment of a separate Minister of Communication, Georges Fillioud, to oversee the change.

The evolution of French broadcasting between 1981 and 1986 was dramatic. The period saw the birth of hundreds of local radio stations and the advent of three private TV channels to complement the three existing state ones. Lang's influence on policy, however, could be described at best as peripheral. The areas of culture and television did overlap at times, however, and certain ideas of the cultural project did appear in the programming requirements, or <u>cahiers</u> <u>des</u> <u>charges</u>, of the state channels as well as in the debate surrounding establishment of France's first private TV stations.

---

* To add to the confusion, the deputies who prepare to reform television are among those French who watch least.

REFORMING THE MONOPOLY

The boom in television in France began in the 1960s, coinciding with the first years of the Fifth Republic. The Gaullists, like previous governments in the 1950s, viewed television as an extension of the state radio monopoly established shortly after World War II. Until 1974, all broadcasting was the responsibility of the Office de la Radio et Télévision Francaise (ORTF). The French government also acquired control or indirect influence over "peripheral" francophone broadcasting operations in Luxembourg, Monte Carlo, and Germany's Saar region. The state monopoly extended not only to broadcasting but to production itself. Some programs were imported, but all French programming was produced by a single entity, the Société Francaise de Production (SFP). Although attempts sometimes were made to maintain "objectivity," the news was generally influenced by the government. After a strike by journalists in 1968 protesting restrictions on coverage of the May riots, de Gaulle's allies at the ORTF fired most of those thought to be Leftist sympathizers. In addition, although Presidents Pompidou and Giscard were a bit less interventionist during the 1970s, most Socialist leaders were convinced that television served as a major support for the Right during the PS's years in opposition. Mitterrand went so far as to accuse Giscard of turning the state monopoly into "his principal instrument of government." (1)
     A number of attempts were made to reform the broadcasting system prior to 1981, but none challenged the idea of a continued state monopoly. The political stakes were too high. Change focused primarily on introducing advertising to finance higher production costs and breaking up the ORTF into smaller units. The system that Mitterrand inherited from Giscard consisted of highly centralized pieces of the old ORTF bureaucracy--three AM radio stations (France Inter, France Musique, and France Culture), three TV channels (TF1, Antenne 2 and the supposedly decentralized FR3), the SFP production company, and a centralized technical broadcasting operation. In addition to questions of control and administration that made the Socialists suspicious of the government role was an added challenge: emerging technologies threatened to make the monopoly untenable. Pirate FM radio stations (radio libres) first began broadcasting in the late 1970s, many with Socialist support. Meanwhile, the existence of satellites and cable technology meant that France could no longer insulate its borders from outside broadcasts.
     The dramatic change in French broadcasting during the Socialist years was thus a product of political desire and technical/economic expediency. The result was perhaps the most open system France has ever known but one which was not yet immune from the political shenanigans so typical of its past.
     Mitterrand's first step in trying to separate the state from direct involvement in broadcasting was to establish a separate authority--the Haute Autorité de l'Audiovisuel--to oversee the system, set rules, and appoint the general managers of the TV stations. Members of the Haute Autorité were chosen for nine-year terms according to the formula used for the Constitutional

Council: three members chosen by the president of the Republic, three members chosen by the president of the National Assembly, and three members chosen by the president of the Senate.   The format,   although   representing   an   important   step   toward independence of the mass media,   gave Socialist appointees six of the nine seats on the Autorité.   In a study commissioned by the British Broadcasting Corporation in December 1985,   author Roland Cayrol concluded,   "It is common knowledge that, on the whole and despite some moments of tension or even crisis. . . the Haute Autorité has   not   shown much independence of action   from   the Government and the President of the Republic." (2)

Despite the Socialist   desire to keep some control over   the media,   not   all   change could be planned.   Realizing   that   the opening of the FM radio band to private stations was inevitable, the government stepped in to organize it.   The July 29, 1982, law establishing the Haute Autorité also legalized the radio libres. However,   the   legislation showed a distinct imprint of Socialist philosophy: commercial advertising was not allowed, and stations were supposed to be operated by civic associations and religious and   community   groups.   Demand   for licenses was so   high   that frequencies   had   to be shared in many   large   cities.   However, Socialist dreams of decentralized radio libres becoming a new source of regional consciousness,   an idea promoted by many after 1968,   have not been realized.   Community groups, from Moslems to homosexuals,   make   broadcasts,   but   by far the most   successful stations   are   those playing rock music.   Although the   law   was intended   to   impede the creation of powerful   FM   networks,   the Paris rock station NRJ built up a series of affiliates throughout France   in   three   short years.   When the   government   tried   to challenge the NRJ network, protest marches by young people forced it to back down. (3)

The   first   changes   on television   took   place,   not surprisingly,   in the news divisions.   An almost complete renewal of personnel took place after 1981,   but journalists--including some Communists for the first time--operated more independently than in the past.   A 1/3-1/3-1/3 rule applied for airing political views,   divided between the government,   the majority parties,   and   the opposition.   (4)   Needless to say,   the Right grew disenchanted with the monopoly once out of power.

Meanwhile,   technology   was on the   march.   Low-frequency pirate TV stations threatened to become as big an issue as the clandestine radio libres had been in the late 1970s. A consortium of European countries was scheduled to launch a new television satellite in 1986 that would open up two new channels for France. The success of a pay movie channel, Canal plus, operated by the government-owned Havas ad agency, was proof that the market could sustain more television.   Mitterrand,   realizing that the   state could ill-afford to finance extra networks and that the Socialist majority was not eternal,   took a gamble and on January 4,   1985, announced   his   support   for   private   television.   Commented L'Express, "Francois Mitterrand does not want to be passed by the Right in the area of liberty." (5)

The public soon learned, however, that Mitterrand was not an altruist.   Having accepted private television as inevitable, the Socialists   reasoned   that they could control it better   if   they

awarded the licenses rather than the Right.   The fifth channel,
La 5, was awarded in November 1985 to a group led by French
businessmen Jerome Seydoux and Christophe Riboud--two friends of
Mitterrand--and Italian TV magnate, Silvio Berlusconi. Following
Italy's move to liberalize television in the 1970s, Berlusconi
built that country's largest network, relying heavily on imported
American movies and serials, as well as game shows.

In order to get the station operating before the March 1986
elections, the government also pushed through a bill claiming
eminent domain over the Eiffel Tower (property of Jacques
Chirac's Paris city government) for the purpose of installing a
powerful transmitter!   In the weeks preceding the election, a
video music channel (TV6) also went on the air.   Opposition
leaders unanimously condemned "Socialist television" as   a
political and cultural farce and promised to destroy it.   After
the elections, the new minister of culture _and_ communication,
Francois Leotard, announced plans to reassign ownership of the
licenses to operate La 5 and TV6 and dropped a bombshell: TF1,
the country's oldest and largest station, would be privatized and
the Haute Autorité dissolved in favor of a new regulatory body
(ostensibly more independent but presumably friendlier to the
Right).

TELEVISION AND THE CULTURAL DEBATE

One of the many ironies of the Socialist period was that
throughout the first years when the government pursued an
interventionist cultural policy and held almost complete control
over the TV networks, there was little attempt to bring the two
areas together.   Only when the debate over private television
began did cultural considerations become a major issue. This was
due to a number of factors.   As already demonstrated, the
information function of television was clearly of   primary
importance to Mitterrand.   Second, most cultural leaders,
including Lang, failed to appreciate the cultural aspects of
television until the threat of a serious deterioration in program
quality became apparent.   The truth was that cultural leaders
rarely took television seriously.   Pierre Cabanne's 500-page
book, _Cultural_ _Power_ _and_ _the_ _Fifth_ _Republic_, does not even
mention television.   While French television was never a model
for objectivity, quality of nonnews programming was generally
high.

> So long as de Gaulle and Malraux remained in charge of the
> spiritual well-being of the French, the ORTF bought little
> of the American pulp material so common on British screens--
> and though French quizzes and variety shows can be as banal
> as any, at least before 1969 they were balanced by twenty to
> thirty hours a week (excluding schools TV) devoted to the
> arts, history, travel, and so on.   The approach was often
> dull and conformist, the editing sloppy. . . but no one
> could deny the high cultural tone. (6)

The introduction of advertising in 1968 and increased

competition between state networks after the breakup of the ORTF
in 1974 forced television to be a bit more responsive to the
public.   The French, like audiences everywhere, showed a taste
for   comedies,   adventure   series,   and movies--all of them
preferably made in the U.S.A.   However, although French
television slowly came to resemble the program mix prevalent
throughout the West, successive governments' stiff requirements
(<u>cahiers</u> <u>des</u> <u>charges</u>) restricted the number of movies shown to
protect cinemas and guaranteed a high level of French production
as well as a minimum number of hours of "cultural" broadcasts
each week. Arts programs rarely appeared in prime time, although
"Apostrophes," a weekly book review program at the start of
Antenne 2's Friday-night lineup, has been consistently one of the
country's top-rated shows.

Some   attempt was made to take advantage of television to
promote Ministry of Culture policies or objectives after 1981,
most notably in the plastic arts, where Mollard sought to educate
the public about contemporary art by coproducing a show about the
Delegation of Plastic Arts' projects.   The show ("Désir des
Arts," Antenne 2, May 19, 1985) got low ratings but increased
news coverage of "events" such as the Paris Biennale, Christo's
wrapping the Pont Neuf, and the Buren affair probably did a great
deal to raise public awareness.

Lang's chief interest in television appears to have been in
linking its future more closely to that of the film production
industry.   His objective was to work around the SFP monopoly,
long attacked as inhibiting creativity on the three state
channels.   The establishment of Canal plus in 1984 and the
arrival of the first independent local cable networks (authorized
by the Haute Autorité) gave the ministry a chance to take a
direct role in television production.   In 1984, the Fonds de
Soutien aux Industries de Programmes, a "transitory mechanism" to
aid the new networks, produced 340 hours of original
programming. (7) In addition, the new SOFICA, private production
companies created by the 1986 tax reform, were authorized to
produce television shows as well as movies.

Although a strong opponent of the state monopoly over
television production, Lang supports continued state ownership of
the networks. The commercial requirements of private stations
mean that the <u>cahiers</u> <u>des</u> <u>charges</u> of all must be modified,
sacrificing the government's ability to impose high levels of
national production or cultural programming.   Loyalty to
Mitterrand impeded(s) Lang from attacking the award of La 5, but
the arrival of Berlusconi's version of unbridled commercialism
and the heavy reliance on American imports to fuel it runs
counter to the goals of the Socialists' cultural project.   The
fifth channel was neither edifying nor creative and had little to
contribute to the Socialist dream of a mutation of society.
Clearly, other political objectives took precedence.

Although the move to accommodate private television was a
blow to cultural advocates, the government promised that they
would not be left out.   While La 5 was given one spot on the new
European TDF 1 satellite, the remaining French spot was reserved
for an exclusively "cultural" channel to be developed in the
future in cooperation with the existing FR3 network.   The

Table 8

<u>French TV Viewers' Preferences, 1982</u>

	% who watch often or from time to time	% wishing more programs of this type
Feature films	87	28
Nature/animal programs	84	15
Variety shows	71	12
Shows about other countries	60	12
Dramas and TV movies	59	7
Medical shows	58	25
Circus	54	8
Sports	49	11
Daily life of French	49	6
Debates/interviews with political figures	48	5
Documentaries on political, economic, and social problems	47	5
Theater	45	8
Science	43	11
History	40	8
Books and writers	39	9
Classical music	22	5
Ballet/dance	21	4
Plastic arts	20	5
Pop, folk, rock, jazz	17	7
Opera	12	2

<u>Source</u>: Ministry of Culture. <u>Développement Culturel</u>, no. 53.

government also budgeted money for the Société Européene de Production de Télévision (SEPT) to coproduce cultural programs with other European television networks. SEPT chairman Bernard Fevre D'Arcier, who ran the Avignon festival from 1981 to 1984, has managed to coax a number of important French theater directors into working for television for the first time. In addition to the cultural benefits, there is an obvious political stake in that the French-sponsored SEPT represents a challenge to the European Community's attempt to build a European television network, something French nationalists on the Left and Right are doubtless appalled by.

In retrospect, it appears that although cultural objectives were minor factors in the evolution of French broadcasting between 1981 and 1986, the Socialists tried to go out ensuring a place for culture in a changed environment. It remains to be seen whether any of the more ambitious aspects of the Socialist blueprint--the cultural channel or the SEPT--survive. However, supporters of culture in France rarely looked to television for guidance before 1981, and it is an open question whether they will in the future. It is hard to escape the fact that with the exception of "Apostrophes" and an occasional concert, even the "cultural constituency" appears to prefer westerns and comedies when watching television (see table 8).

NOTES

1. Mitterrand, _Ici_ _et_ _Maintenant_, p. 99.

2. Roland Cayrol, "Problems of Structure, Finance, and Programme Quality in the French Audiovisual System." Paper prepared at the request of the Peacock Committee of the BBC, December, 1985, pp. 2-3.

3. Ghislaine Ottenheimer, "Radio-télé: ouverture et tour de vis," _L'Express_, January 18, 1985, p. 35.

4. Cayrol, p. 10.

5. Ottenheimer, p. 35.

6. Ardagh, _The_ _New_ _France_, p. 615.

7. _La_ _Politique_ _Culturelle,_ _1981-1985_, "L'audiovisuel et le cinéma," p. 9.

5
Architecture
and the Politics
of Grandeur

Il se prend pour Ramsès II, le President?*

<u>L'Evénement</u> <u>du</u> <u>Jeudi</u>, June 26, 1986

Despite the activities of the Ministry of Culture in every artistic sector, the Socialist commitment to culture will best be remembered not by the mixed legacy of rhetoric and hard work left by Lang, but by the enormous monuments in Paris with which President Mitterrand decided to mark his term in office. The <u>grands</u> <u>projets</u> represent an expenditure of more than 15 billion francs in a time of economic crisis, and their thrust is decidedly cultural: a popular opera at the Bastille, a science and music "city" at La Villette, a completely renovated Grand Louvre, the Orsay Museum of nineteenthth-century art, and the Institute of the Arab World. The new Ministry of Finance, one of the two noncultural projects, was necessitated by the Grand Louvre project; even the Tête de la Défense, a Parisian world trade center, has been billed as a crossroads for international communication.

The <u>grands</u> <u>projets</u> quickly became an essential part of the broad Socialist concept of "culture" which, according to Roger Planchon, is no longer understood. Noted MIT urban studies professor Julia Trilling, "While the French Socialist government has yet to find a formula for translating its commitment to culture into a stream of literary or artistic <u>chefs-d'oeuvre</u>, it can build temples to culture." (1)

More surprising, perhaps, than the willingness of the French state to commit itself to such an ambitious program was the pivotal role of Mitterrand not only in proposing the overall plans but in supervising their execution down to the smallest

---

* Does the President take himself for Ramses II?

details.   Even those projects that originated with Giscard, such
as the Orsay Museum, the science museum,   and the Institute of
the Arab World, received the Mitterrand touch.
     The "Mitterrand style" is less an idea of what a city should
look like and more an idea of what a city should be.   In terms
of architecture, the projects display a range of diversity
consistent   with   the Socialist commitment to   encouraging
individual expression. "We do not have a preestablished model,"
wrote Lang in <u>L'Architecture Aujourd'hui</u>.   "French society is
pluralist   today;   sensibilities,   aspirations,   tastes   are
different, often contradictory." (2)   As part of the commitment
to pluralism, foreign architects also were invited to submit
designs.   While the projects will work as a group to transform
the appearance of the capital and round out most of its less
developed edges, they are united principally by function--culture
and communication--rather than form.   As such, they represent a
clear political and cultural statement about France's direction
in the 1980s.
     Supporters and critics alike point to the "fait du prince"
in architecture as a uniquely French prerogative in today's West.
In Germany and Italy monumentalism is synonymous with past
Fascism, while in Britain and the United States expensive, bold
architectural   statements   are   associated   with   corporate
headquarters rather than public buildings. (3)   The presidents
of the Fifth Republic, like the old kings of France, have a
unique opportunity to leave their mark on style. President
Pompidou was the first to turn his attentions to a cultural
institution.   The inside-out, high-tech style of the modern art
center that bears his name has made the building a Paris
landmark.   In addition to establishing a precedent for ambitious
cultural "temples," the Pompidou Center also demonstrates a
uniquely French ability to take a comprehensive (and expensive)
approach to cultural planning.   Instead of single-use concert
halls and museums,   the French build "centers" incorporating
libraries, public spaces, and research functions. Mitterrand's
<u>grands</u> <u>projets</u> thus set out to do for the ensemble of French
culture what the Pompidou Center has accomplished for modern art.
     Although French presidents have each had pet projects, none
had as many as Mitterrand, nor did any expect to get them
completed before the end of their term.   These two factors make
the <u>grands</u> <u>projets</u> stand out and explain the profound influence
they had on shaping all of French cultural policy.   They explain
how a government which took office promising an innovative,
decentralized approach to culture and the money to pursue it was
slowly consumed by the needs of large, Paris-based institutions--
a process that in the future could threaten the most important
objectives of the Socialist cultural project.

COOPERATION AND COHABITATION

The success of the <u>grands</u> <u>projets</u> required cooperation from a
number of people whose support was not inevitable.   Within the
government, Lang's role was crucial.   As construction got
underway, the Ministry of Culture's financial contribution grew

at the expense of other priorities. Many Direction heads and administrators expressed dissent, but the fact that the internal debate never went public is a testament to Lang holding the ship together. Only Maurice Fleuret could be counted as an unwavering supporter of the projects. The Bastille Opera won him a great deal of credit in the music world, and, although it took up a large chunk of his budget, he used the project to justify continuing expenditures for commissions (for new works) and music schools (to train more singers for the projected demands of the new opera).

The most critical and prickly support had to come from Mayor Jacques Chirac and his staff of cultural advisers at the Paris city hall. As the unofficial opposition leader, Chirac was in principle against "Socialist" monuments, but the mayor showed a pragmatic approach to the whole affair. Anyone studying a precedent for the Left/Right cohabitation in government that emerged after the Socialists lost the March 1986 legislative elections need look no further than the grands projets. One of Chirac's most cherished dreams was to fill in the few areas of the capital that remained undeveloped. Inasmuch as the grands projets represented the possibility of revitalizing blighted areas with the national government picking up the tab, the city raised few objections. Mitterrand's proposal to continue work on the science museum at La Villette and add a "city of music" drew little protest from Chirac, who was eager to clean up the rundown area around the old abattoirs. In the case of the Institute of the Arab World, Lang responded to the city's objections to an already approved site in the 15th Arrondisement by seeking the advice of the influential Ateliers parisien d'Urbanisme and eventually choosing a different location. (4) Similarly, Mitterrand gave the city government a boost by agreeing to build the new Ministry of Finance at Bercy, the focus of city efforts to develop the rotting quais at the eastern end of the city behind the Gare de Lyon. Officials of the powerful ministry had proposed a location on the more fashionable western side of the capital. (5)

When Chirac and his advisers objected to projects, they did surprisingly little to obstruct their progress. All municipal permits for construction and survey work were granted. "As a legal entity we did not intervene," said one member of the mayor's staff. "As a political entity hostile to the government. culture." The mayor facilitated changes in the zoning process for the Bastille Opera even though he objected strongly to the cost, particularly the projected operating expenses.

Perhaps the most interesting area of Left/Right cohabitation and the grands projets is the plan to build a Grand Louvre Museum. Few objected to the need to renovate the old Louvre palace, whose facilities were extremely poor for a major world museum. Mitterrand took complete control of the project. Architects for most of the grands projets were chosen through competitions, but for the Louvre no selection process took place. Without consulting anyone, Mitterrand chose Chinese-American architect I. M. Pei, famous for his design of the east wing of the National Gallery in Washington. Pei visited Paris a number of times and met with the president secretly before his plan was unveiled.

When announced, Pei's idea sent shockwaves across France and the entire world. He called for radically restructuring the floorplan of the palace by installing a subterranean lobby beneath the Louvre courtyard. Above the new entrance would be a giant glass pyramid, lying directly within the famous axis running from the Louvre through the Tuileries Gardens up the Champs Elysées and ending at the Arc de Triomphe. Art critics on the Left greeted the proposal as a symbol of progress, even genius. The outcry on the Right was tremendous. Mitterrand (with the help of a non-French architect!) was destroying Paris; the pyramid was the height of Socialist arrogance, and so on. (6) With publications such as the influential Le Monde on its side and Chirac's staff prepared to fight, the Right could have turned the issue into a major political showdown. However, after examining a model of the project and meeting with the architect, the mayor quieted the entire controversy by giving the pyramid his support. Construction began on schedule.

WINNERS AND LOSERS

Unlike other cultural programs, the grand projets are more a domain of the presidency than a policy area of the Ministry of Culture, to which most are assigned. As such, the life of the grand projets goes beyond the 1981-1986 time frame established for the rest of this book and extends at least to the end of Mitterrand's presidency, scheduled for 1988. Although the conservative government that took office in March 1986 under Chirac's leadership as prime minister has pruned back the scale of some of the projects, it appears that the grands projets as a package will survive (with the possible exception of the Bastille Opera). The public also seems to approve of the grands projets by a ratio of nearly 3:1. (7) The accomplishment of so vast a cultural infrastructure represents an enduring statement about the Mitterrand era and the commitments of the modern Socialist party.

It is too soon, however, to tell if the grands projets will play host to the new culture and new audiences that were the more abstract goals of the Socialist culture policy. If anything, there is considerable fear that the president's ambitious building program may have negative affects on other Socialist cultural goals. Perhaps the most significant consequence of the grands projets was a shift of resources back to Paris. Construction costs are temporary, but the largely uncalculated future expenses for personnel, security, maintenance, and heating of the new or expanded institutions will make it difficult to return to the promise of decentralization and help for local cultural policies implicit in Lang's first budgets. Although cultural spending increased each year between 1981 and 1986, spending on the grands projets grew from about 15 percent of the budget to nearly 70 percent. The Senate report on the 1986 budget noted that the ministry had lost its "margin of maneuver" between the needs of institutions and those of artists.

> The logic of the [grands projets]. . . thus opens on a
> paradox: despite the strong growth of the budget, the state
> will, in time, only be able to assure the financing of a few
> large cultural institutions. (8)

The biggest casualty in the battle over cultural credits
caused by the grands projets was decentralization. The line in
the 1986 budget dedicated to decentralization fell a dramatic 50
percent from 1985, passing from 126 million francs to 63 million.
The Développement Culturel division saw its credits cut by nearly
25 percent under Lang's last budget. Direct subsidies to local
governments and "associations" also fell 10 percent. (9)

Meanwhile, while culture in the provinces and its devotées
appear to lose from the grands projets, working-class and middle-
income Parisians do not seem to be getting much benefit from them
either. By revitalizing older neighborhoods, the projects appear
to be accelerating the gentrification of the capital. Just as
already happened in the Halles District around the Pompidou
Center, long-time residents of the Bastille area and the 19th
Arrondisement around La Villette are being forced out.

Alain Billon, the former deputy for the 19th Arrondisement,
predicted his own defeat in the 1986 elections three years early.
The reason: the changes in his constituency as a result of
construction at La Villette. Unfortunately for Billon, he was
caught between two unfriendly bureaucracies, Paris city hall and
the Elysée. He blamed the mayor's office for encouraging a
working-class exodus by refusing to evict squatters from
abandoned buildings in the area, thus quickening the pace of
deterioration and subsequent gentrification. He blamed the
Mitterrand administration for having interests that did not
coincide with those of the neighborhood or its residents. "The
new projects must serve those who already live in the
neighborhood," said Billon in 1983. "The neighborhood is going
to be inundated." (10)

Complaints from cultural boosters in the provinces, critics
in the National Assembly and Senate, and artists themselves did
little to stop the building projects. For the Socialists, the
importance of the grands projets lies in the statement that they
will make to Paris, the nation, and the world. "We must show
that we are capable of doing this," said Lang. (11) Adding
2,000 seats will never make an opera "popular," and most visitors
to the enlarged Louvre probably will be foreign tourists, just as
today. However, the grands projets will serve as a testament to
Lang's own idea that "a combative, independent culture belongs to
a living society," a society the Socialists feel they worked to
create.

NOTES

1. Julia Trilling, "Paris: Architecture as Politics," The
Atlantic, October 1983, p. 26.

2. As quoted in Chaslin, p. 33.

3.   Jean-Louis Pradel, "Petite histoire des grands projets," L'Evénement du Jeudi, June 26, 1986, p. 74.

4.   Chaslin, p. 143.

5.   Ibid., p. 102.

6.   Ibid., pp. 122-124.

7.   Catherine Bezard, "Il se prend pour Ramsés II, le Président?" L'Evénement du Jeudi, June 26, 1986, p.77.

8.   Sénat. Commission des Finances, du Contrôle Budgétaire et des Comptes Economiques de la Nation. Rapport Générale (no. 96) sur le projet de loi des finances pour 1986, adopté par l'Assemblée Nationale, Tome III, Annexe no. 7, "Culture," November 21, 1985, p. 9.

9.   Ibid., p. 14.

10.   Alain Billon, personal interview with author, Paris, June 21, 1983.

11.   Jack Lang, "L'Heure de Vérité," Antenne 2 TV.

6
The End of the Monopoly

Dans ce pays pétri par l'histoire et dont la politique est faite de mémoire, de récurrence et de symboles, tout ce qui se joue sur le terrain des idées--et qui nourrit la politique--influence directement la vie sociale.*

Max Gallo, government spokesman, Le Monde, July 26, 1983

Until 1981, the Left--and, more generally, the PS--appeared to hold a comfortable monopoly over cultural and intellectual life in France. Once Mitterrand took office, however, an entirely different picture began to emerge. Middle-class members of the cultural constituencies became preoccupied with other factors, such as the deteriorating economic situation. Meanwhile, the political opposition, which initially supported Lang's request for funds, was quick to attack. A report of the Senate Finance and Budgetary Control Commission dated November 22, 1982, underlined many of the points that discomforted the ministry's critics. Spending, the report charged, was increasing in all areas with little regard for setting priorities. Use of increased funding was not being properly monitored in certain areas, particularly theater, cinema, and architectural projects. Furthermore, the report accused the ministry of _dirigisme_: distributing decentralization credits as a function of ideas "à la mode Rue de Valois [referring to the ministry's Paris address]" rather than of regional cultural objectives; imposing too many regulations on the "cultural industries"; and ignoring the possibilities of corporate patronage. The commission also raised objections to the emphasis of the ministry's international

---

* In this country, moulded by history, where politics is made of memories, recurrences and symbols, everything that involves the plane of ideas--and that nourishes politics--directly influences social life.

activity: "Without wishing to negate the importance of Latin
America and the Mediterranean basin, we hope to see 'l'action
internationale' orient itself equally toward North America and
Europe." (1)
     More   alarming for the Socialists was the fact that,
disregarding the increased budget, which received unanimous
support, the ministry's policies engendered a great deal of
discontent in the artistic and intellectual communities.   Some
were upset about the ministry's growing power, others because
they did not receive aid they expected.   Still others were
disillusioned with the Socialists' entire approach to cultural
affairs.   One of Lang's more hostile critics, former Ecole des
Beaux Arts director Jean Musy, has gone so far as to say, "The
Left was elected just as its ideas went out of fashion." (2)
     The great wave of intellectual and artistic support that the
PS expected never really materialized.   If anything, artists
tended to be uncomfortable with the Socialist experience.   In a
1984 interview, filmmaker Jacques Bral explained why a new wave
of French films featured the darker, marginal side of life
(sadistic or brutal homosexuality, incest, drugs):

> Before May 10, 1981, crime and police movies reflected a
> certain   reality. They   were often critical in nature--
> housing and financial scandals, etc. Now, the future
> appears more somber, since the remedies have failed. Thus,
> there is a pessimist vision in the movies: the marginal
> becomes the heroic. (4)

     The political orientation of the intellectual class, so
often thought to be firmly Socialist, appeared to be far more
complicated.   Furthermore, it became evident that the Right,
perhaps taking a cue from the PS, was increasingly interested in
culture at all levels.   As the 1983 municipal elections
approached, the Right was determined to challenge the Socialists
on all fronts.   In short, in just two years   much of the
theoretical and political basis for the Socialist cultural
project was shattered.

THEORETICAL MISCONCEPTIONS

On July 26, 1983, _Le Monde_ initiated a month-long series of
articles under the rubric "The Silence of the Intellectuals of
the Left."   The theme sparked a great deal of interest and debate
because, in a sense, it underlined the weakness of the
government's ideological and cultural aspirations.   As the
satirical weekly _Le Canard Enchaîné_ put it, "Les intellectuels,
quand ils se taisent, qu'est-ce qu'il fait comme bruit, leur
silence!"4
     "Has the Left abandoned its ideas?" asked government
spokesman Max Gallo in an editorial that initiated the series.
(5) Gallo lamented the growth of "ideas on the Right" coinciding
with the Socialist victory in 1981, but he reserved his greatest
concern for the withdrawal of most of the post-1968 intellectuals
from active political debate.   The Socialists' distress at the

lack of intellectual support reflected their long-held assumption
that, just as intellectuals had helped shape much of their
opposition platform, so would they participate wholeheartedly
with the PS once it was victorious; a replay of 1936. "The stake
is clear," wrote Gallo. "Under the direction of new political
classes will the country effect the mutation that imposes itself,
as much on the economic as social level." (6)

A few artists and intellectuals did take up important
positions in the Mitterrand administration, particularly writers,
with whom the president enjoys a strong rapport. However, their
decisions in no way represented a broad class movement. The
Socialists discovered that the blanket support of the
intellectuals could not be taken for granted. Writer Régis
Debray, sometime revolutionary and one of Mitterrand's closest
advisers, commented, "It is a little less chic now to be on the
Left." (7) As revealing as it is, Debray's remark only skims
the surface of two questions that should have been posed by the
Socialists years before. What is the nature of the French
intellectual community, and what is the extent of its political
commitment?

Division on the Left

Ever since World War II, French intellectual and cultural
life has been characterized as "Leftist" by all types of
commentators--journalists, sociologists, politicians, and members
of the affected communities themselves. However, as Philippe
Boggio pointed out in a followup to Gallo's article, the generic
term "de gauche" implies "a conglomerate of furious
individualism, a social class that cannot be classified, a tiny
minority in number, but an arch-majority through its influence on
national history." (8) Rebelling against the narrow philosophical
guidelines of Communism in the late 1960s, the intellectuals and
artists may have formed a natural cultural constituency for the
resurgent PS, but they never were an "organic" part of a larger
Socialist whole, at least not in the Gramscian sense.

As long as the parties of the Left remained in opposition,
the hard questions did not have to be asked. The Socialists,
eager to foster unity of the non-Communist Left, assumed a
natural cohesion between the new intellectuals and the ideals of
the PS. Mitterrand and his associates came to believe that the
intellectuals were behind the PS, the "cultural project," and the
plan for a peaceful "mutation" of society. "Do men of culture
and science now turn toward the PS?" an interviewer asked
Mitterrand in 1980. "I wish that were true," he replied. "It
increasingly is." (9)

However, the Socialists failed to see the divisions between
their political aspirations and those of the intellectuals, or
the divisions among the intellectuals themselves. Contrary to the
Fascist threat of the 1930s, few intellectuals on the Left saw
any overriding reason to close ranks in the 1980s. Jacques
Cellard, a linguist, captured this sense in an article entitled
"A Certain Bad Conscience." He wrote, "Happily, neither the
Church, nor the Army, nor even racism do not sufficiently weigh

on France in 1983 to merit an organized resistance of spirit that is the vocation and the raison d'être of intellectuals." (10)

Some intellectuals told Le Monde that they continued to openly support Mitterrand. (11) Catherine Clément, a writer who was in charge of artistic and cultural exchanges at the Foreign Ministry, defended the PS policy in the following way: "The state's only duty is to provide the material conditions to make thought possible. . . . It is up to each person to choose, within this open space, his own distance as regards the state power." (12) However, the consensus of most intellectuals who contributed their thoughts throughout the month was harsher. "Since May 1981, Big Brother tells us, 'The state dreams for you!" wrote Jean-Edern Hallier. (13) "In essence," wrote philosopher Henri Lefèbvre in response to Max Gallo, "you wish for an intellectual avant-garde that will politically fight for you." (14) Echoing Cellard, Lefèbvre added that there was no place for an avant-garde without an adversary, and "the American way of life" was not it.

According to Boggio, the PS's greatest mistake was ignoring the views of the nouveaux philosophes, such as André Glucksman and Bernard Henri-Lévy, leading thinkers of the 1970s who were moving rapidly away from Marxism. From the beginning, these men denounced "'the archaic ways of the Socialists,' the 'socialo-poujado-populist' style of the Pantheon ceremony, and the 'cultural protectionism' of M. Jack Lang.'" (15) Furthermore, Boggio continued, the presence of Communists in Mitterrand's government, even as junior partners, became a source of hostility from intellectuals as well as others. "In power, the Left is suspected of complaisance toward the East and of a guilty weakness toward the Communists. What was only a combat of the nouveaux philosophes in June or September became the affair of a majority of intellectuals in December 1981, with the state of emergency in Poland." (16) While the Socialists did become increasingly hostile toward the Soviet Union and the opposing attitudes of their Communist junior partners, the decision to let the Communists remain in the government as long as possible (the PCF withdrew in 1984) cost them much support.

Politics, Culture, and the New Right

The breakdown in relations between the Socialist Party and a large number of its former sympathizers in the intellectual and artistic communities gave the PS serious problems. The intellectuals may have had trouble finding a political adversary, but the PS could easily detect a cultural one in the form of resurgent Right-wing politicians. After years of neglect, culture--its objectives and administration--became an important issue for the opposition during and after the March 1983 municipal elections.

Although not as well organized as PS efforts, culture had never been an entirely dead issue on the Right. While the Giscard administration contributed little to cultural progress, Presidents de Gaulle and Pompidou valued the projects of the Ministry of Culture, although low priority was given to culture

in the national budget. Perhaps the most successful new cultural
institution in the last few decades, the Pompidou Center, was due
largely to the special efforts of the late president. However,
as Jacques Rigaud had pointed out in the mid-1970s, the Right
rarely had thought of cultural policy in purely political terms.
In 1983, this was no longer true.

The new breed of Right-wing politicians accepted cultural
programming as an essential part of good government, and, as
their socialist counterparts discovered earlier in the 1970s,
they realized that voters rewarded cultural efforts. A L'Express
study of municipal life prior to the 1983 elections showed many
opposition cities, such as Caen, Orléans, and Bordeaux, alongside
such Socialist and Communist powerhouses as Grenoble, La
Rochelle, and Le Havre in the designation of the top ten cities
for cultural life. (17)

While many provincial mayors, most notably Bordeaux' Jacques
Chaban Delmas, can be cited as culture boosters, the undisputed
leader of the Right's new use of culture was and remains Jacques
Chirac in his capacity as mayor of Paris. After being elected in
1977, Chirac quintupled the capital's cultural budget (to
approximately $75 million), made culture one of three top
priorities (along with housing and stopping crime), and explained
that "'culture must become a habit if Paris is to become a
creative city again.'" (18)   Chirac assembled a large staff of
cultural advisers, including Jean Musy, the former director of
the Ecole des Beaux Arts who was fired by Jack Lang.   In their
eagerness to reanimate the city, Chirac's advisers have looked to
traditional Parisian street life and new innovations from as far
away as New York.   During the 1970s, encroaching modernity--in
the form of skyscrapers, superhighways, and long commutes--
threatened Paris's reputation as a center of cultural vitality.
Today, Chirac has restored a great deal of civic pride through
his programs, from a city marathon to an arts festival during the
normally dormant summer months (the Festival Estival) to concerts
in the Metro stations--all announced on large electronic
signboards spread throughout the city.

Surprisingly, Chirac sports few intellectual credentials.
He is, however, a consummate politician who recognizes the value
of a commitment to culture.   At the outset of his abortive run
for the presidency in 1981, he wrote, "It is not wrong, on the
eve of such a decisive date, to remember. . . that culture is
also en jeu [part of the game]." (19)

Since the arrival of Mitterrand and Lang, Chirac entered
into a constant war with the Socialists over the development of
cultural policy and the grands projets in Paris. The mayor and
his staff jockeyed to get the most for the city out of the
government's ambitious building plans, while the Socialists
fought to keep any credit for improvements in Paris from going to
the opposition leader.   The division went much deeper than
assigning responsibility for architectural projects, however.
While both sides had similar policy goals in terms of
revitalizing French culture and bringing the arts closer to
people's everyday lives, a wide gap of theory and politics
divided them, one that Chirac most effectively exploited.
Borrowing perhaps more from the Left than from the Right, Chirac

fully endorses the concept of culture as a political question. However, he seeks a cultural policy that "conforms to the Gaullist idea of an individual and collective civic conscience, assuring perennial national values as well as continued progress towards greater liberty and solidarity." (20)   This theory is, of course, in contrast with the Socialist long-range conception of culture as a vehicle for mutation and social change.

CULTURE AT THE POLLS

The 1983 municipal elections, the first test of the Socialists' strength following their 1981 legislative victory, provided a perfect opportunity for Chirac and his allies to carry the cultural squabble beyond Paris. Rightist publications such as Le Figaro and Le Figaro Magazine (different editorial board) stepped up their attacks on Lang, from his extensive contacts with leaders in Cuba and Eastern Europe to his flamboyant life-style. Le Figaro Magazine cultural editor Patrice de Plunkett hastily published a vicious personal attack on Lang, La Culture en Veston Rose, with aid from the conservative Table Rond organization. (21)   As the elections approached, local cultural budgets and policies were of major interest, and cultural life was an essential part of preelection analyses in many major publications. "No one disagrees anymore that a large part of the municipal budget must go for culture," said Le Matin. "The argument is over the utilization of these enormous sums." (22)
In Paris, Chirac won reelection overwhelmingly, but he received his highest marks in all polls for his cultural and beautification efforts. (23)   At the other end of the political spectrum, the Socialist mayor of La Roche-sur-Yon, in office since 1977, credited his own reelection to his extensive and popular cultural programs, including restoring the city center and building what L'Express called the best library system in France. (24)   In other Socialist municipalities where mayors could not point to successful mainstream programs, however, culture proved to be a liability.
In communities where campaigns were more heated, uses (and abuses) of cultural policy were widely debated. Young challengers, mostly members of Chirac's RPR movement, consistently emphasized the dangers of culture being dominated by the Left, lumping Socialists and Communists together. Specifically, the opposition charged that local governments and the ministry (through the Développement Culturel program) were subsidizing a network of Leftist-oriented associations, enterprise committees, and "Amicales Laiques" that had infiltrated every aspect of cultural life. Lang's heavy-handed policies toward the Maisons de la Culture, where appointments and extra funding were controlled from Paris, became an especially hot topic in many communities. According to Lang, the Maisons de la Culture--the cornerstone of Malraux's policy--were a largely unsuccessful experiment that could only be transformed by placing a "strong personality" in charge, capable of changing them from within.   "If the structure resists, it must be dissolved," he claimed, noting that this was exactly what he did in giving the

Maison de la Culture of Nanterre over as a theater to the director Patrice Chereau. (25)

Nowhere did culture become more politicized than in the city of Nantes. After being elected mayor in 1977, Socialist Alan Chenard appointed an aggressive cultural aide, Jocelyn Cailleau, who laid out an ambitious program of action culturelle-- increasing spending, buying up available theaters for the city, and attacking "elitist" cultural institutions. After May 1981, with the arrival of Lang and Dominique Wallon at the Ministry of Culture, funds flowed easily, with Paris's contribution rising from 4,156,000 francs in 1981 to 11,193,000 francs in 1982. (26) Cailleau asked Lang to replace the director of the Maison de la Culture, Loic Volard, well known for his ability to attract top artists to the city. As the socialist-oriented Le Matin described the issue, "It is true that there was a different conception of culture [at Volard's theater]. . . And it is also true that the municipality wished to see the Maison de la Culture open to local potential and to become creative." (27) According to Volard, "Cailleau wanted a political theater. I said: no. She mounted mock public consultations... to accuse us of complicity in 'bourgeois culture.' And the municipality brought Paris into the game." (28) Volard did not leave Nantes. The city and the Ministry of Culture only contributed half the budget, with the opposition-controlled regional council providing the rest. The region diverted its support to Volard, building him a new theater, while, to quote Le Matin, "another conception of culture" reigned at the Socialist-backed Maison de la Culture.

The "two cultures" debate was bound to be a leading issue in the 1983 elections. Senator Michel Chauty, the RPR challenger, accused his opponent of mismanagement and wasting funds on cultural programming of little interest to the town. As proof that "Socialist culture" was inappropriate, Chauty cited an avant-garde play called Bas Ventre with the theme of defecation, a production subsidized by the city government. Among his campaign slogans: "Quelle Culture pour Nantes? La Merde!" The Socialists defended their policies of independent "creation" and support for regional culture. Chauty defeated Chenard and cut off the town's subsidy to the Maison de la Culture as one of his first acts, effectively closing it. Commented Chenard, "The assault taken against the Maison de la Culture hits a city that was awakening to culture and that was beginning to have a coherent policy in that domain." (29) Paris's response was to pour extra money into the cultural budgets of more cooperative suburban communities.

Chauty's move in Nantes was followed by other new RPR mayors in former Socialist (as well as Communist) municipalities throughout France. In Brest, where a situation of polarization similar to Nantes existed, the new mayor tore up the city's "cultural contract" with the ministry and cut off funding to the Maison de la Culture, an affiliated radio station and numerous associations judged to be politically biased. Right-wing editor Plunkett, who spearheaded many attacks on Lang's cultural policies in the pages of Le Figaro Magazine, promised, "What was alive will not disappear. What was artificial will." (30)

In those communities where Socialist mayors were challenged

but held onto power, cultural policies came under pressure for change as well. In Rennes, a Socialist/Communist coalition ran city government since 1977. As part of a new cultural policy, the director of the Maison de la Culture, Chérif Kaznadar, was named to direct the municipal theater as well. As programming changed from a range of classical operas to include more contemporary compositions, attendance declined and an association of opera buffs was formed to charter buses to classical performances in other cities. The Socialist mayor narrowly won reelection and, cognizant of the criticisms leveled at his program during the campaign, set about changing the town's cultural administration to be more responsive to the public. Kaznadar resigned (he was appointed director of the Maison des Cultures du Monde in Paris), and his successor is none other than the former head of music programming, who had been replaced in 1977! In addition, the town reduced its subsidy for the annual Festival des Arts Traditionnels, a pet project of Kaznadar's wife. (32)

No matter how much they objected to Lang's policies, however, few mayors were willing to cut their ties to the ministry and its money. In Avignon and Grenoble, two "model" Socialist cities lost to the RPR, the mayors were more selective and concentrated on getting rid of politicized associations (although Avignon mayor Jean-Pierre Roux did fire the director of the municipal theater, the son of the former PS mayor). Most mayors were emboldened by the 1983 campaigns to demand--and obtain--more autonomy in their dealings with Paris, resulting in an uneasy cooperation in which both sides tried to get the upper hand. Lang could claim correctly that, barring a few cases such as Nantes and Brest where mayors sought to make political capital by fighting him, most cities continued to follow the lead of the ministry. At the same time, as RPR mayor of Epinal Philippe Seguin pointed out, "Is not the best way to combat Lang to take his money?"32

Although substantial disagreements continued between many municipalities and the Ministry of Culture, they declined in political significance after 1983. Raymond Barre and Giscard's former minister of culture, Michel Guy, attempted to revive the issue in October 1985 by sponsoring a colloquium in Lyon to address "state cultural imperialism," but the initiative failed to gather momentum. Indeed, as the 1986 elections approached, it was the Socialists who once again tried to earn political capital from culture.

Rather than emphasize specific policies, the Socialist approach to culture in 1986 centered on Lang and his image as a culture booster. In his five years in politics, Lang had come to represent an idea of culture that went well beyond any criticisms leveled at the ministry. Artists who complained about restricted credits or the ministry's growing bureaucracy rarely blamed their problems on Lang. For those with enough stature to command the minister's attention, or the chance to encounter him during one of his numerous visits throughout the country, Lang was seen as accessible and open to different points of view. For all members of the cultural community, Lang was personally responsible for the giant boost in cultural spending since 1981; where the money went was an administrative issue separate from Lang himself.

Most important for the Socialists in 1986 was the positive public perception of Lang and what he was trying to achieve. Right-wing candidates used culture effectively as a political weapon in 1983 because they were able to focus on problems with individual institutions, such as a local Maison de la Culture or opera. However, once attention turned to the national level, voters did not appear to be very interested in changing the direction of cultural policy or the state's active role. Two polls taken in the autumn of 1983 revealed some surprising results considering the polemics of the previous months. In a survey conducted by Louis Harris for the Left-leaning _Le Matin_ (December 7, 1983), 87 percent of respondents agreed that the state should take an interest in culture, and the number rose to 93 percent for municipal governments. More important, the Socialists received about a 50-percent rating of "good or "very good" for overall cultural programs in the Harris survey and in a poll conducted by the SOFRES organization for the conservative _Le Figaro_ (December 7, 1983). Also surprising was the support for expanding the ministry's activities toward newer cultural areas and new publics (see tables 9 and 10). (33)

With the knowledge that the public approved of the ministry's broad objective to expand cultural offerings and opportunities, Lang switched tactics and embarked on an aggressive public relations program to link the Socialists with the future of cultural policy. Ideological goals of building a new society by linking culture with larger political objectives were no longer mentioned. Instead, Lang emerged as the PS's strongest cultural asset--a man roving the country helping projects large and small get off the ground. He attended festivals in the provinces and presented models of the new cultural projects in Paris that would restore French leadership in the arts while bringing culture closer to the people. At daily press conferences, he showed just how much more was planned.

The message was clear: Without the Socialists and Lang there would be no cultural policy. As the elections approached, numerous Socialist-leaning publications characterized the situation as "L'enjeu culturel," literally, the cultural stakes.

The bonds that held the cultural constituency together were no longer strong enough, however. The real battles--for sufficient funding, recognition of new art forms, and "excluded" artists and publics--already were won. What remained was a host of smaller issues that sometimes divided people bitterly and more often caused considerably less excitement. Although politicians took different stands on specific issues from television to the Buren columns, neither the Communists on the Left nor the RPR/UDF on the Right proposed to change radically the direction of cultural policy.

What a difference five years meant! Thanks to Lang, the "cultural stakes" were minimal.

Table 9

Harris Survey
(December 1983)

The state should try to increase public access to cultural
institutions in the following social categories:

Category	% Responding Affirmatively
Youths	98
Handicapped	98
Rural residents	95
Immigrants	84

Source: Le Matin.

Table 10

SOFRES Poll
(December 1983)

Do you find the activities of the ministry justified in the
following sectors?

Sector	% Responding Affirmatively
Circus	80
Popular music	79
Comic strip	69
Rock music	65
Fashion	59

Source: Le Matin.

NOTES

1.   Sénat. Commission des Finances, du Controle Budgétaire et des Comptes Economiques de la Nation. <u>Rapport Général</u> (no. 95, sur le projet de loi de finances pour 1983, adopté par l'Assemblée Nationale. Tome III, "Les Moyens et les Dispositions Spéciales," pp. 3-4.

2. Jean Musy, personal interview with author.

3.   Francois Forestier, "Les Bas-Fonds de la Série Grise," <u>L'Express</u>, March 23, 1984, pp. 8-9.

4.   Dominique Durand, "Cherchez la Gauche," <u>Le Canard Enchaîné</u>, August 10, 1983, p. 8.

5.   Max Gallo, "Les Intellectuels, La Politique et la Modernité," <u>Le Monde</u>, July 26, 1983, p. 7.

6. Ibid., p. 7.

7. As quoted in Philippe Boggio, "Le Silence des Intellectuels de Gauche," <u>Le Monde</u>, July 27, 1983, p. 1.

8. Ibid., p. 6.

9. Mitterrand, <u>Ici et Maintenant</u>, p. 162.

10. Jacques Cellard, "Une Certaine Mauvaise Conscience," <u>Le Monde</u>, August 6, 1983, p. 6.

11.   Henri Guillemin, "Oui Sans Commentaires," <u>Le Monde</u>, August 5, 1983, p. 7; Vercors, "Pas Décus, Patients," <u>Le Monde</u>, August 6, p. 6; Catherine Clément, "Choisir sa Propre Distance," <u>Le Monde</u>, August 10, 1983, p. 6.

12. Clément, p. 6.

13.   Jean-Edern Hallier, "L'Avènement du Tiers Etat Culturel," <u>Le Monde</u>, August 10, 1983.

14. Henri Lefèbvre, "La Crise des Avant-Gardes," <u>Le Monde</u>, August 6, 1983, p. 6.

15. Boggio, p. 6.

16. Ibid., p. 7.

17. "Municipalités: Où Vit-on le Mieux?" <u>L'Express</u>, February 11, 1983, p. 64. Unfortunately, the methodology used in the study does not provide an entirely fair picture. Measurements of "amount of money spent" in a given area or "rates of frequentation" favor large cities over smaller ones in determining the general classifications. Thus, smaller cities with active cultural programs may be classified below larger ones

that have made lesser efforts.

18. Justine de Lacy, "Cultivating Culture in Paris," New York Times Magazine, May 22, 1983, p. 43.

19. Jacques Chirac, preface to Pierre Emmanuel, Culture, Noblesse du Monde (Paris: Editions Stock, 1980), p. 10. It should be noted that, in addition to the politicians and journalists mentioned here, a small group of nouvelle droite philosophers is trying to make itself a place on an intellectual and cultural scene dominated by the Left since World War II. One of the major leaders of this group is Alain de Benoist, publisher of the journal Eléments. The cover story of the summer 1983 issue of the journal, entitled "La Culture Gadget," provides an interesting, ultranationalistic opinion about the state of French culture and cultural policy.

20. Ibid., p. 10.

21. Patrice de Plunkett, La Culture en Veston Rose (Paris: La Table Rond, 1982).

22. "Les voix de la Culture, Dimanche au Fond des Urnes," Le Matin, March 5, 1983, p. 20.

23. de Lacy, p. 52.

24. Sylvie Pierre-Brossolette, "Gauche: Rares Bonnes Surprises," L'Express, March 18, 1983, p. 54.

25. As quoted in Colette Godard, "'C'est le Choix des Personnes Qui Guide D'abord nos Actions,' Nous Déclare le Ministre de la Culture," Le Monde, July 19, 1983, p. 15.

26. Patrice de Plunkett, "Les Nouveaux Maires d'Opposition Contre la Culture de Gauche," Le Figaro Magazine, July 2, 1983, p. 44.

27. "L'Opposition à l'Assaut des Maisons de la Culture," Le Matin, June 30, 1983, p. 8.

28. As quoted in de Plunkett, "Les Nouveaux Maires. . .," p. 44.

29. As quoted in Jean-Pierre Bedei, "La Culture dans le Collimateur R.P.R.," L'Unité, June 3, 1983, p. 5.

30. Patrice de Plunkett, personal interview with author, Paris, June 22, 1983.

31. Philippe Urfalino, L'Allocation de ressources sans critères de choix: La mise en oeuvre des politiques culturelles municipales. Thesis for doctorat in sociology, 3eme cycle. Fondation Nationale des Sciences Politiques/Institut d'Etudes Politiques de Paris, 1984, pp. 310-315.

32. Sibylle Mignon, "Opposition: les maires préparent l'après-Lang," _Le Point_, October 21, 1985, p. 72.

33. _Le Matin_, December 7, 1983.

Conclusion
The House That
Jack Built

Il fallait dépasser l'image d'une culture vécue en marge du quotidien, comme un "supplément d'âme," voire un luxe, et considérer la vie culturelle non comme un domaine privé mais comme une chose publique.*

Jack Lang, <u>Après</u> <u>Demain</u>, February 1986

The March 1986 elections produced a change of majorities and marked an end to Lang's tenure at the Ministry of Culture. It is an open question whether the same date marks the end of the Socialists' cultural project. Many policymaking aspects of the project survive, as do the policymakers themselves. Abirached remains director of theater, and Fleuret continues as head of the direction of music. Claude Mollard has established a private consulting business, advising both left- and right-wing mayors on how to animate their cities. After much controversy, the <u>grands projets</u> appear headed for completion with the exception, perhaps, of the Bastille Opera. Lang, now a deputy representing the rural department of Loir et Cher, continues to speak out authoritatively on cultural issues, more so than his successor. He continues to maintain his network of contacts across the country and build his image as a national cultural leader through <u>Allons-z-idées</u>, his personal political/cultural "movement."

Yet, from an ideological standpoint, the cultural project is finished. The question is whether it even survived until 1986. Politically, a number of the Socialists' most innovative policies suffered enormous setbacks after the early years. Interventionist actions such as the book price regulations were resented by many; the "anti-American" criticism and the presence

---

* It was necessary to go beyond the image of an aged culture at the margin of daily life, as a soul soother, a luxury, and consider cultural life not as a private domain but as a public thing.

of Communists in the government alienated other would-be supporters as well. Most important, the Socialists strayed farther and farther away from the initial objectives of decentralization and aid for municipal cultural policies--the very issues on which they had identified their interest in culture throughout the 1970s.

Culture no longer "belonged" to the Socialists as an issue, and this not only threatened the PS's continued control of its cultural constituencies but also challenged the use of culture as a source of legitimacy for the party. The mixed bag of theoretical concepts developed by the Socialists, when put to the test, did not hold. Intellectuals openly resisted being considered an organic class, ready to establish a new hegemony. Cultural policies of action/développement culturel that moved too far into the ideological arena were opposed by the electorate and many artists as well. Journalist John Vinocur noted in 1983, "The French government's experience has become the example of what the Left in Spain and Italy do not want to do." (1)

It is, however, unfair to call the PS' cultural experiment a failure. Due largely to the efforts (and mistakes) of the Socialists, culture has earned a place near the top of the political agenda in France, even during a period of severe economic difficulties. As France became more modernized and better educated, more urban and less rural, people were bound to place a greater value on culture. This fact formed the basis for the phenomenal adhesion of the cultural constituencies to the PS in the 1970s. It also lies behind the Right's more recent decision to adopt the cultural issue as well. Following Chirac's reelection, Le Monde noted, "It was the Mayor's forte to have realized long before anyone else that culture would be to the 1980s what ecology was to the 1970s." (2) While the analogy is correct, one might wish to award the credit to the many Socialist leaders who launched this movement during the 1970s itself but failed to realize its true nature.

Unlike the Gramscian/Popular Front concepts of culture as a precursor of social change, support for cultural policy in the 1970s and 1980s came because society already had changed. The traditional opposition of conservative beaux arts supporters and Communist intellectuals was no longer a valid representation of French society; the Socialists had stumbled onto fertile ground. Pascal Ory writes in the introduction to his unique cultural history of France between the two Mays (1968 and 1981), "Essentially, the political victory of 1981 was that of a socializing culture, or still social-democratic, over Communist culture. . . in France for the first time in fifty years." (3)

What is remarkable was that with the victory won, the Socialists had so little success in controlling future developments. Despite its millions, the Ministry of Culture does not seem to have gained any leverage in determining the tastes or habits of the French. Its effectiveness in any area of the arts would appear to be conditioned on a measure of prior public acceptance. Thus, Fleuret's innovative music policies won praise because France was in the midst of a revival of interest in music while Mollard's equally innovative policies met with ambivalence at best from a public that was not ready to understand or

appreciate contemporary art. Also, while the Socialists may have
increased   the volume of cultural output, they do not   seem to
have   influenced   its content.   In areas as   diverse   as
architecture,   theater,   the plastic arts,   and television,   the
1980s   have produced no recognized style in France beyond a
celebration of diversity.

The Lang years are thus a testament to the success of a
policy and the decline of an ideology. While culture may never
prevail as a source of political legitimation for the Socialist
party, the Socialists successfully have legitimized cultural
policy.   Earlier governments paid lip service to culture and all
the while kept funding to a minimum.   Mitterrand pledged not to
turn his back on culture and he did not. The result: srprisingly
widespread   interest   in cultural   policy   and   subsequent
disagreement as to how it should be administered.

It may have required a Socialist administration to raise
cultural spending and consciousness, but it did not take long
for others to adopt the issue. For the most part, the cultural
constituency,   rather than seeking to be part of an avant-garde,
wants effective, nonideological policy administration. The fact
that culture has received so much attention in recent election
campaigns thus may eventually help cultural policy move away from
ideological and sectarian goals, a first step toward
concentrating on actual improvement in French artistic life for
amateurs and professionals alike.   Ironically, by becoming a
competitive issue on all sides, as opposed to the quasi-monopoly
of one, future support and development of the arts and culture in
France may be strengthened.

Justine de Lacy writes, "The thing that's cheering up many
Parisians these days is the prospect of watching Left and Right
jump through hoops as they try to help the City of Light live up
to its legend." (4)

LESSONS OF THE FRENCH EXPERIENCE

From the outset, this study examined two major factors--policy
and ideology--in terms of three broad categories: the depth of
change from an elitist to a popular culture; the interaction of
cultural innovation and the bureaucratic phenomenon; and the
political objectives of Socialist cultural policy. Each category
feeds into the next, and a final look at the whole they create
reveals that beneath the successes and the failures, France has
moved into a new era.

The transition from elitist to popular culture was probably
the brightest spot of the cultural project.   There is no denying
that the activities of the Ministry of Culture touch the lives
and interests of more French citizens today than was the case in
1980.   More important, this was accomplished without depriving
classical or contemporary artists of additional credits and
attention.   A subtle change in emphasis had occurred, however.
Democratization was achieved not by tearing down walls, as Leo
Lagrange had proposed in 1936, but by enlarging the park.

The philosophy of the Popular Front, adopted by Malraux,
revolved around using the state to open up access to classical

culture for all. However, rather than concentrate on removing the barriers that separate the vast majority of the public from understanding and enjoying traditional culture, the Lang ministry concentrated on legitimizing popular practices, thus recognizing the existence of separate elite and popular cultures and only reducing the distinction previously drawn between them.   Thus, overnight, millions of Frenchmen were told that, without changing their tastes or habits, they were vital contributors to the nation's cultural life. However, while the French experience provides an excellent lesson in how to make people feel they are part of their government and society, it is disturbing that most French remain out of touch with some of their country's greatest artistic traditions and achievements.   In this respect, little has changed in the past five years.

A final aspect of the first question is whether the Socialist cultural leaders did not themselves constitute a new elite.   Lang was and remains the true representative of the so-called "intellectuels de gauche," Socialist sympathizers ranging from actual creators and cultural administrators to young professionals with personal interests in the arts. However, the power and cohesiveness of this group as a cultural elite is probably overestimated.   What appeared to be a monolithic group in the 1970s, all wearing round, rimless glasses and clutching dog-eared copies of the Nouvel Observateur, turned out to be an unpredictable constituency in the 1980s.   The disagreements voiced at Avignon between artists and government officials as early as 1981 and the "silence of the intellectuals" of 1983 revealed a class characterized by dissension and debate--which is, in fact, what the Socialists had claimed they wanted.   The irony was that once debate was opened it did not always lead to the kind of blanket support many Socialists naively assumed it would bring about.

For those who supported the intent of the cultural project, its greatest weakness was one of administration, not ideas. Bureaucracy has been a strength and scourge of modern France, and its functioning was paramount in shaping the evolution of the Ministry of Culture during the boom years.   With the dramatic growth in the budget, the expansion of bureaucracy was inevitable.   The best job administrators such as Lang, Fleuret, and Abirached could do was make themselves more accessible to counter its presence.

Under the circumstances, it is hard to imagine that decentralization even could have been imagined in France much less gone as far as it did after 1981. Despite the disappointing reconcentration of government attention and spending in Paris in the final years, there are a few signs that the cultural bureaucracy has proved more flexible than that of other ministries.   Administrators, many of whom were once local officials, accepted the idea of support for varied, small-scale initiatives rather than endorsing grandiose and disappointing projects such as the Maisons de la Culture.   The problems that arose were more over issues of control than policy itself.   The emergence of cooperation on the regional level, an area where politicians and bureaucrats see mutual benefits, has been one of the most exciting developments and could serve to break the

stalemate between local interests and the ministry.
     Did the Socialists make any political capital out of their
cultural policy?   This is the final question in the ideology vs.
policy debate.   Perhaps the most striking development of the
cultural policy was how closely it followed the evolution of
other government policies.   In 1981, Lang's cultural crusade and
separation of "light from darkness" symbolized the new beginning
that Mitterrand and the Socialists promised in all areas of
society.   As   time went on and government bywords became
productivity and modernity, Lang's themes changed toward "economy
and culture" and the promise of the <u>grands</u> <u>projets</u>.   Wrote <u>La</u>
<u>Croix</u> cultural editor, Jean Lebrun, "Culture, at each stage, was
presented as an indispensable tool of general policy." (5)
     Was this then the political role of the cultural project--to
make the ideal only a mirror of the real? The Socialists clearly
did not change society, nor did they dramatically alter patterns
and forms of cultural expression in France.   Yet, so much seems
to be different about the mood of French culture and society in
the late 1980s than that which prevailed at the beginning of the
decade.
     The cultural policy, while not producing any significant art
movement or achieving any specific goal such as decentralization,
appears to have conditioned people to think in a new way about
themselves and the options facing their country. Lang proved that
the   most important element to policy was the concept of
partnership.   In almost every area, he used government funds as a
catalyst but sought to build an alliance with others.   Lang's
most important partnerships were the direct relationships he
developed with artists on one side and the public on the other.
Although individual policies sometimes came under attack, the
essential trust that existed between the ministry and these
groups was never questioned and allowed Lang to remain an
activist through his last months in power and beyond.
     The   notion of partnership was also critical to the
introduction of new concepts into French cultural life. <u>Mécénat</u>
was at last accorded serious attention by the ministry and the
French public in general.   This is a fundamental acknowledgment
of the fact that private agents have an important role in
supporting and enhancing cultural life.   The rise of private
radio and television is also an acceptance of this notion, no
matter how many doubts on quality are expressed.
     The final area of real partnership created by the cultural
policy is the relationship between local government and the
Ministry of Culture.   While complete decentralization will
probably never take place in France, it should be noted that
cultural policy remains a fundamentally local issue.   Ever since
Malraux launched the Maisons de la Culture, the national
government has tried to recognize the need to extend cultural
activities into the provinces.   The Lang ministry elevated
cooperation to a new priority, and, although falling far short of
the mark and actually regressing in later budgets, it raised a
new consciousness that is shared by Socialist and right-wing
mayors alike.
     It is perhaps due to the growing sense of partnership that
culture in France is at last breaking out of the paralysis into

which   politics   had   placed   it.   Until 1981,   artists and
intellectuals   maintained   an   adversarial   relationship   with
government   even   as they became increasingly dependent upon it.
After the Socialist victory,   the political justification for the
hostility   disappeared: "the arrival of the Left was   identified
spontaneously, even ideologically, with an end to oppression over
creation,   thus   over   creators." (6)   The   experience   of   the
ensuing years separated artists from the myth of a utopian Left
but   taught   them   how to work with officials   to   achieve   their
goals.
     The challenge for Lang's successors is to extend further the
hand of partnership and to keep established relationships with
artists, the public, and local government open.

AN AMERICAN PERSPECTIVE

France's historical and intellectual tradition, sociological
makeup, and government structure all contribute to a unique
politics of culture.   However, the debate over cultural policy is
of major concern in Europe and the United States as   well.   Many
of the elements that contributed to the phenomenal rise of
cultural constituencies in France--growth of universities, a
better-educated urban population--can be found throughout the
West.   William J.Baumol and William G.   Bowen noted two decades
ago   that   "the minority of the [American] public that is
interested in the arts is endowed with a disproportionate share
of the nation's social,   economic, and political power." (7)   The
rapid advance toward what some sociologists term postindustrial
society suggests that there will be an even larger audience for
the arts and one with more time to enjoy them.   Despite all of
these factors,   France in the early 1980s was alone in its drive
toward a well-funded cultural policy.   From Reagan's America to
much of Western Europe,   government subsidies for the arts were
cut as the welfare state fell on hard times.   The New York Times,
noting this trend,   even made the point that the decreasing role
of government cultural funding was the true wave of the future in
the cultural area. (8)
     Can anything be learned from the French example,   or should
it be dismissed as inapplicable or anachronistic?   Even the most
casual American observer would find little in common between the
two societies in the area of cultural policy.   Happily,   culture
in   the   United States carries neither the political   nor
ideological baggage that weights down many of France's better
efforts.   Furthermore,   culture   in   America   is   truly
decentralized.   While New York may claim a leadership position
among the nation's cities,   it does not rival Paris as a focus of
the nation's cultural and ideological life.   Across America,
funding for the arts comes from a variety of sources, sometimes
public,   more often private.   The "consumer" pays a large share
(certainly more than in France),   and, thanks to a tradition of
patronage and tax incentives,   corporate support for the arts is
an old and significant factor in the United States, whereas it is
only a recently discovered and limited option in most European
countries, including France. Most important, the American system

is characterized by a sense of local initiative and broad public and private concern for the arts.

The opposite side of the American coin, however, is that the arts continually find themselves in a squeeze for funds. In their 1966 hallmark study, _Performing Arts--The Economic Dilemma_, Baumol and Bowen underlined a continuing "income gap" for the arts in the United States, in spite of increases in productivity through new technologies and projected rises in individual and corporate support. However, while the French have discovered Baumol's law that spending has its limits while demands are infinite, the arts in France do not suffer the kind of financial pressures that occur in even the most prestigious American institutions. Large-scale government subsidies, to some extent, may affect the dynamic of private initiative and concern that exists in the United States, but the idea that good culture only comes as a result of a Bohemian starving in an attic no longer holds in today's world. With the reductions in grants from Washington during the Reagan years, the consequences of the income gap are more acute than ever. A front page article in The _New York Times_ in 1984 told the story:

> Leaders of many of the nation's major nonprofit theaters, faced with continuing financial problems, say they are making artistic compromises to remain solvent. This retrenchment affects an informal network of theaters that has produced virtually all the major American dramas and many musicals for the last decade. (9)

In a sense, one is left with the feeling that the grass is always greener on the other side. American artists, administrators, and the cultural public envy the French because of their financial commitment. For the French, however, mired in ideology and tradition, America's innovative dynamism and decentralized participation are obvious sources of envy.

In the best of all possible worlds, France and America could teach each other a great deal about how to approach cultural policy. To do so, however, requires an understanding of each nation's politics of culture -- the unique pattern of history and social and artistic tradition that is as much a reflection of an entire society as any other measure.

NOTES

1. John Vinocur, "Socialist Governments in Europe Find Intellectuals' Ardor for Left Cooling." _New York Times_, December 2, 1983, p. 12.

2. As cited in de Lacy, p. 52.

3. Pascal Ory, _L'entre-deux mai_ (Paris: Editions du Seuil, 1983), p. 14.

4. de Lacy, p. 53.

5.   Jean Lebrun, "Entre socialisme et féodalisme, le ministère danse," <u>Esprit</u>, March 1984, p. 48.

6.   Jean-Michel Nidaj, "Le Ministère de la Culture: L'Histoire d'une Legitimité," <u>Après</u> <u>Demain</u>, February 1986, p. 6.

7.   William J. Baumol and William G. Bowen, <u>Performing Arts--The</u> <u>Economic</u> <u>Dilemma</u> (New York: The Twentieth-Century Fund, 1966), p. 404.

8.   "Across Western Europe, Cultural Subsidies are Declining," <u>New</u> <u>York</u> <u>Times</u>, January 30, 1984, p. C11.

9.   Samuel G. Freedman, "Financial Problems Are Compromising Nonprofit Theaters," <u>New</u> <u>York</u> <u>Times</u>, March 14, 1984, p. 1.

Bibliography

BOOKS

Adamson, Walter L. Hegemony and Revolution: A Study of Antonio Gramsci's Political and Cultural Theory. Berkeley: University of California Press, 1980.

Ardagh, John. France in the 1980s. Harmondsworth, Middlesex, England: Penguin Books, 1982.

__________. The New France: A Society in Transition. Harmondsworth, Middlesex, England: Penguin Books, 1973.

Aron, Raymond. La Révolution Introuvable. Paris: Librairie Arthème Fayard, 1968.

Attali, Jacques. Bruits. Paris: Presses Universitaires de France, 1977.

Baumol, William J., and Bowen, William G. Performing Arts--The Economic Dilemma. New York: The Twentieth-Century Fund, 1966.

Beaunez, Roger. Politiques Culturelles et Municipalités. Paris: Les Editions Ouvrières, 1985.

Bensaid, Georges. La Culture Planifié? Paris: Editions du Seuil, 1969.

Bonetti, Paolo. Gramsci e la Società Liberaldemocratica. Roma: Laterza, 1982.

Borella, Francois. Les Partis Politiques dans la France d'Aujourd'hui. Paris: Editions du Seuil, 1981.

Bourdieu, Pierre, and Passeron, Jean-Claude. Les Héritiers: Les Etudiants et la Culture. Paris: Les Editions de Minuit, 1964.

Bourricaud, Francois. Le Bricolage Idéologique. Paris: Presses Universitaires de France, 1980.

Brown, Bernard E. Socialism of a Different Kind: Reshaping the Left in France. Westport, Conn.: Greenwood Press, 1982.

Cabanne, Pierre. Le Pouvoir Culturel Sous la Ve République. Paris: Olivier Orban, 1981.

Chalumeau, Jean-Luc. L'art au présent. Paris: Union Générale d'Editions, 1985.

Chaslin, Francois. Les Paris de Francois Mitterrand. Paris:
     Gallimard, 1985.

Clément, Catherine. Rêver Chacun Pour l'Autre. Paris: Librairie
     Arthème Fayard, 1982.

Codding, George A., Jr., and Safran, William. Ideology and
     Politics: The Socialist Party of France. Boulder, Colo.:
     Westview Press, 1979.

de Brebisson, Guy. Le Mécénat. Paris: Presses Universitaires
     de France, 1986.

__________________. Données sur le Mécénat d'Entreprise en
     France en 1985. Paris: Ministére de la Culture Service des
     Etudes et Recherches, 1986.

de Plunkett, Patrice. La Culture en Veston Rose. Paris:
     Editions de la Table Rond, 1982.

Emmanuel, Pierre. Culture, Noblesse du Monde. Paris: Editions
     Stock, 1980.

__________________. Pour Une Politique de la Culture. Paris:
     Editions du Seuil, 1971.

Friedberg, Erhard and Urfalino, Philippe. La Décentralisation
     Culturelle: La Culture au Service des Régions. Paris:
     Ministère de la Culture. 1984.

Gaudibert, Pierre. Action Culturelle: Intégration et/ou
     Subversion. Paris: Casterman, 1971.

Goldmann, Lucien. La Création Culturelle dans la Société
     Moderne. Paris: Denoel, 1971.

Gramsci, Antonio. The Modern Prince and Other Writings, Louis
     Marks, trans. New York: International Publishers, 1980.

Gramsci e la Cultura Contemporanea, II. Roma: Editori Riuniti--
     Istituto Gramsci, 1970.

Heinrich, Natalie. Les Artothèques. Paris: Ministère de la
     Culture, 1985), p. 46.

Hemmings, F. W. J. Culture and Society in France, 1848-1898. New
     York: Charles Scribners Sons, 1971.

Inglehart, Ronald. The Silent Revolution. Princeton: Princeton
     University Press, 1977.

Jaurès, Jean. L'Esprit du Socialisme, Ferrier, Jean-Louis, ed.
     Paris: Editions Gouthier, 1964.

Jeanson, Francis. L'action culturelle dans la cité. Paris: Editions du Seuil, 1973.

Joll, James. Three Intellectuals in Politics. New York: Harper & Row, 1960.

Lang, Jack. L'Etat et le Théatre. Paris: Librairie Générale de Droit et de Jurisprudence, 1968.

__________, and Jean-Denis Bredin. Eclats. Paris: Jean-Claude Simoen, 1978.

Leon Blum, Chef du Gouvernement 1936-1937. Paris: Librairie Armand Colin, 1967.

Maier, Charles S. Recasting Bourgeois Europe. Princeton: Princeton University Press, 1981.

Mesnard, André Hubert. La Politique Culturelle de l'Etat. Paris: Presses Universitaires de France, 1974.

Miège, Bernard, et. al. L'Appareil d'Action Culturelle. Paris: Editions Universitaires, 1974.

Mitterrand, Francois. Ici et Maintenant. Paris: Librairie Arthème Fayard, 1980.

Mollard, Claude. Le Mythe de Babel. Paris: Grasset, 1984.

__________. La Passion de l'Art. Paris: Editions de la Différence, 1986.

Ory, Pascal. L'entre-deux mai. Paris: Editions du Seuil, 1983.

Petit-Castelli, Claude. La Culture à la Une. Paris: Club Socialiste du Livre, 1981.

Piotte, Jean-Marc. La Pensée Politique de Gramsci. Paris: Editions Anthropos, 1970.

Portelli, Hugues. Gramsci et le Bloc Historique. Paris: Presses Universitaires de France, 1972.

Programme Commun de Gouvernement du Parti Communiste Francais et du Parti Socialiste. Paris: Editions Sociales, 1972.

Projet Socialiste Pour les Années 80. Paris: Club Socialiste du Livre, 1981.

Puaux, Paul. Les Etablissements Culturels (Rapport au Ministre de la Culture, March 1982). Paris: La Documentation Francaise, 1982.

Queyranne, Jean-Jack. _Les Régions et la Décentralisation Culturelle_ (Rapport au Ministre de la Culture, July 1982). Paris: La Documentation Francaise, 1982.

Reynaud, Jean Daniel and Grafmeyer, Yves, eds. _Francais, Qui Etes-vous?_ Paris: La Documentation Francaise, 1983.

Rigaud, Jacques. _La Culture Pour Vivre_. Paris: Gallimard, 1975.

Ritaine, Evelyne. _Les Stratèges de la Culture_. Paris: Presses de la Fondation Nationale des Sciences Politiques, 1983.

Safran, William. _The French Polity_. New York: David McKay Co., 1977.

Sagot-Duvauroux, Dominique. _Le Role de la Subvention au Théâtre_. Paris: Université de Paris I--Pantheon Sorbonne. Doctoral Thesis.

Salamini, Leonardo. _The Sociology of Political Praxis_. London: Routledge & Kegan Paul, 1981.

Suleiman, Ezra. _Elites in French Society_. Princeton: Princeton University Press, 1978.

UNESCO. _Statistical Yearbook_. Various issues. Paris: United Nations Education and Scientific Organization.

Urfalino, Philippe. _L'Allocation de Resources sans Critères de Choix: La Mise en Oeuvre des Politiques Culturelles Municipales_. Paris: Fondation Nationale des Sciences Politiques, 1984. Doctoral thesis.

Ziebura, Gilbert. _Léon Blum et le Parti Socialiste, 1872-1934_. Duplex, Jean, trans. Paris: Librairie Armand Colin, 1967.

ARTICLES

"Across Western Europe, Cultural Subsidies are Declining." <u>New York Times</u>, January 30, 1984, p. C11.

"André Malraux S'Explique," <u>Le Nouvel Observateur</u>, October 14, 1978, p. 7.

August, Thomas G. "Paris 1937: The Apotheosis of the Popular Front." <u>Contemporary French Civilization</u>, vol. v, No. 1, Fall 1980, pp. 43-60.

Bedei, Jean-Pierre. "La Culture dans le Collimateur R.P.R." <u>L'Unité</u>, June 3, 1983, pp. 4-5.

Besancon, Alain. "Culture: de la révolution à l'animation." <u>L'Express</u>, March 7, 1986, p. 34.

Bezard, Catherine. "Il se prend pour Ramsés II, le Président?" <u>L'Evénement du Jeudi</u>, June 26, 1986, pp. 76-77.

Boggio, Philippe. "Le Silence des Intellectuels de Gauche." <u>Le Monde</u>, July 27, 1983, p. 1.

Casanova, Jean-Claude. "Télévision: le chemin de la liberté." <u>L'Express</u>, February 28, 1986, p. 29.

Cayrol, Roland. "Problems of Structure, Finance, and Programme Quality in the French Audiovisual System." Paper prepared at the request of the Peacock Committee of the BBC, December 1985, photocopy.

Cellard, Jacques. "Une Certaine Mauvaise Conscience." <u>Le Monde</u>, August 6, 1983, p. 1.

Clark, Priscilla. "Literary Culture in France and the United States." <u>American Journal of Sociology</u>, vol. 84, no. 5, March 1979, pp. 1057-1077.

Clément, Catherine. "Choisir sa Propre Distance." <u>Le Monde</u>, August 10, 1983, p. 6.

"Création et consommation musicales: le grand écart," <u>Esprit</u>, March 1984, pp. 51-62.

"Culture Descends from Its Pedestal," <u>Economist</u>, January 9, 1982.

de Lacy, Justine. "Cultivating Culture in Paris." <u>New York Times Magazine</u>, May 22, 1983, pp. 42-53.

de Plunkett, Patrice. "Les Nouveaux Maires d'Opposition Contre la Culture de Gauche." <u>Le Figaro Magazine</u>, July 2, 1983, pp. 42-48.

Dévarrieux, Claire. "Nouveaux Départ." Le Monde des Arts et des Spectacles, June 11, 1981, p. 16.

Dionne, E. J., Jr. "Culture Meeting in Paris Sets Off Debates." New York Times, February 21, 1983, p. C9.

Dumur, Guy. "Un Utopiste du Possible." Le Nouvel Observateur, March 4, 1978, p. 79.

Durand, Dominique. "Cherchez la Gauche." Le Canard Enchaîné. August 10, 1983, p. 8.

"Enquête: Culture Année Zéro." Le Quotidien de Paris, April 11, 1983, p. 29.

Fallot, Evelyn. "La Folie de la Musique." L'Express, February 2, 1982, pp. 56-64.

Forestier, Francois. "Les Bas-Fonds de la Série Grise." L'Express, March 23, 1984, pp. 8-9.

Freedman, Samuel G. "Financial Problems Are Compromising Nonprofit Theaters." New York Times. March 14, 1984, p. 1.

Fumaroli, Marc. "De Malraux à Lang: l'excroissance des Affaires Culturelles." Commentaires, Autumn 1982, pp. 247-259.

Gallo, Max. "Les Intellectuels, La Politique et la Modernité." Le Monde. July 26, 1983, p. 7.

Georges, Michèle. "Télé: les chaines du Président." L'Express, November 29, 1985, pp. 14-16.

Gilbert, Claude. "Biaiser avec la politique: L'activité culturelle à Grenoble." Esprit, March 1984, pp. 86-98.

Godard, Colette. "'C'est le Choix des Personnes qui Guide D'abord nos Actions' Nous Déclare le Ministre de la Culture." Le Monde, July 19, 1983, p. 1.

Gournay, Bernard. "Un Ministère de la Culture: L'Expérience Francaise." Administration Publique, no. 22, September 1982.

Gout, Etienne et al. "La Politique Sociale du Front Populaire" in Léon Blum, Chef du Gouvernement, 1936-1937. (Paris: Librairie Armand Colin, 1967), p. 275.

Grand, Georges. "Une Grève Pour la FNAC?" Le Monde, August 7, 1981, p. 2.

Guyaz, Jacques. "Innovations dans le secteur des services: du militant à l'entrepreneur," in Francais, Qui Etes-vous? (Paris: La Documentation Francaise, 1981), pp. 191-201.

Hallier, Jean-Edern. "L'Avènement du Tiers Etat Culturel." Le Monde, May 21, 1981, p. 16.

Holleaux, André. "La Politique Culturelle Francaise." Administration Publique, no. 22, September 1982.

Lebrun, Jean. "Entre socialisme et féodalisme, le ministère danse." Esprit, March 1984, pp. 48-50.

Lefèbvre, Henri. "La Crise des Avant-Gardes." Le Monde, August 6, 1983, p. 6.

"L'enjeu culturel." Après-Demain, no. 281, February 1986, pp. 2-39.

"L'enjeu de Société n'est pas Politique, Mais Culturel, déclare M. Jacques Attali." Le Monde, May 21, 1981, p. 16.

"L'Etat et les Galeries d'Art." Canal, no. 56/57, Summer 1984, pp. 10-14.

"L'Opposition à l'Assaut des Maisons de la Culture." Le Matin, June 30, 1983, pp. 6-8.

Lhomeau, Jean-Yves. "L'Avenir de la Gauche et la Bataille Culturelle." Le Monde, July 8, 1983, p. 1.

Lindon, Matthieu. "Préférez Vous Faulkner ou SAS?" Le Nouvel Observateur, August 8, 1981, p. 60.

"Mainmise sur la Culture?" Esprit, March 1984, pp. 45-110.

Mignon, Sibylle. "Opposition: les maires préparent l'après-Lang." Le Point, October 21, 1985, pp. 71-73.

Mitterrand, Francois. "Un Choix Culturel." L'Unité, May 10-16, 1974.

"Municipalités: Où Vit-on le Mieux?" L'Express, February 11, 1983, pp. 53-68.

Musy, Jean. "La Culture en Cage." Le Figaro, June 16, 1983.

Ottenheimer, Ghislaine. "Radio-télé: ouverture et tour de vis." L'Express, January 18, 1985, pp. 33-35.

Passeron, André. "La Nouvelle Assemblée Nationale Compte Plus de Fonctionnaires Mais Autant d'Elus Locaux que la Précédente." Le Monde, August 8, 1981, p. 6.

Piemme, J. M. "L'action culturelle dans tous ses états." Théâtre-Public, no. 42, November 1981, p. 20.

Pitts, Jesse R.   "Les Francais et L'Autorité." Francais, Qui
    Etes-vous?   (Paris: La Documentation Francaise, 1981), pp.
    285-300.

Pradel, Jean-Louis.   "Petite histoire des grands projets."
    L'Evénement du Jeudi, June 26, 1986, pp. 74-75.

Régent, Claude.   "Une Année de Transition pour Roger Planchon."
    Le Monde, September 17, 1981.

Righini, Mariella.   "En Avant la Musique."   Le Nouvel
    Observateur, January 2, 1982, pp. 44-47.

Saez, Guy. "Politique de Style, Politique de Ville (Grenoble et
    Rennes devant la Culture). Cahiers de l'Animation, no. 43,
    1983, pp. 53-89.

Schneider,   Pierre.   "Beaubourg: Chefs-d'oeuvre sous
    Surveillance." L'Express, March 2, 1984, pp. 6-8.

Simonot, Michel.   "Avignon 81: Un Révélateur." Théâtre-Public,
    xi-xii, 1981, p. 58.

Texier, Jacques. "Gramsci in Francia." In Gramsci e la Cultura
    Contemporanea II, pp. 371-379.

Trilling, Julia.   "Paris: Architecture as Politics."   The
    Atlantic, October 1983, pp. 26-35.

"Un Entretien avec M. Jack Lang." Le Monde, September 5, 1981,
    p. 8.

Vinocur, John.   "Socialist Governments in Europe Find
    Intellectuals' Ardor for Left Cooling." New York Times,
    December 2, 1983, p. 12.

___________________. "Will French Culture Be More French?" TNew York
    Times, January 9, 1983, sec. 2, p. 1.

FRENCH GOVERNMENT DOCUMENTS

Assemblée Nationale. Commission des Affaires Culturelles, Familiales et Sociales. Avis (no. 471). Tome IV, "Culture." October 16, 1981.

Assemblée Nationale. Commission des Affaires Culturelles, Familiales et Sociales. Rapport (no. 252), relatif au prix du livre. July 30, 1981.

Assemblée Nationale. Commission des Finances, de l'Economie Générale et du Plan sur le Projet de loi de Finances pour 1986. Rapport (no. 2987). Annexe no. 11, "Culture." October 28, 1985.

Délégation des Arts Plastiques. "Les Conseillers Artistiques Régionaux," undated.

Direction de l'Administration Générale. Service du Personnel et des Statuts. Bureau de la Formation Continue. Connaissance du Ministère de la Culture, Edition 1983.

Ministère de la Culture. "A Propos de la Chanson Francaise," by Pascal Sevran, 1982.

Ministère de la Culture. Bureau du Budget. "Comment Mesurer l'Impact des Subventions?" by H. Lequien, 1981.

Ministère de la Culture. Direction du Développement Culturel. La politique culturelle en région: Bilan de la léglisature 1981-1985. 1986.

Ministère de la Culture. Projet de loi de Finances, 1983

Ministère de la Culture. Projet de loi de Finances Pour 1983. "Presentation du Budget sous Forme de 'Budget de Programmes.'" Paris: Imprimerie Nationale, 1982.

Ministère de la Culture. Rapport au Parlement sur l'Application de la Loi du 10 Août 1981 Relative au Prix du Livre et sur la Politique du Gouvernement en Faveur du Livre et de la Lecture.

Ministère de la Culture. Rapport de la Mission de Reflexion et des Propositions sur le Cinéma. November 3, 1981.

Ministère de la Culture. Service des Etudes et Recherches. Développement Culturel, numbers 43-65.

    "L'Action Culturelle dans la Commune." December 1979.
    "Pratiques Culturelles et Patrimoine." December 1980.
    "Repères Budgétaires Pour la Culture." September 1981.
    "L'Edition des Livres de 1974 à 1980." December 1981.

"Avignon 81; Les Publiques du Festival." March 1982.
"Les Francais et le Livre." October 1982.
"Les Francais et la Musique." December 1982.
"Les Dépenses Culturelles des Communes." April 1983.
"Les centres dramatiques nationaux." March 1984.
"Les dépenses culturelles des villes." August 1984.
"Les pratiques culturelles des jeunes." April 1985.
"Economie du spectacle vivant." May 1985.
"Les dépenses culturelles des départements." September 1985.
"Les dépenses culturelles des villes 1978-1984." March 1986.

Ministère de la Culture.   Service des Etudes et Recherches.
     Développement Culturel: livres et articles parus en 1981.
     Paris: La Documentation Francaise, 1982.

Ministère de la Culture.   Service de Presse et d'Information.
     "Bilan de l'Activité du Ministère de la Culture Depuis Juin
     1981." May 1982.

Ministère de la Culture.   Service de Presse et d'Information.
     "France, une ambition nouvelle pour la culture," 1982.

Ministère de la Culture.   Service de Presse et d'Information.
     "Intervention de Monsieur Jack Lang, Ministre de la Culture,
     France." Mexico City, July 27, 1982.

Ministère de la Culture.   Service de Presse et d'Information.
     Le Dossier du Mois:

     "La Politique du Livre." no. 1. June 1982.
     "72 Mesures Pour la Création Artistique." No. 2. Oct. 1982.
     "Budget 1983: Les Grandes Orientations." No. 3. Nov. 1982.
     "La Nouvelle Politique du Cinéma." No. 4. March 1983.
     "La Nouvelle Politique du Théâtre." No. 5. April 1983.

Ministère de la Culture.   Service Information et Communication.
     "2 Ans de Politique Culturelle, 81-83."

Ministère de la Culture.   Service Information et Communication.
     "Les Francais Interrogés sur la Politique Culturelle." Le
     Dossier: Sondages, no. 8. January 1984.

Ministère de la Culture.   Service Information et Communication.
     La Politique Culturelle 1981-1985: Bilan de la Legislature,
     1986.

Sénat. Commission des Finances, du Controle Budgétaire et des
     Comptes Economiques de la Nation. Rapport Générale (no.
     58), sur le projet de loi des finances pour 1982, adopté par
     l'Assemblée Nationale. Tomes I. November 23, 1981.

Sénat. Commission des Finances, du Controle Budgétaire et des
     Comptes Economiques de la Nation. Avis (no. 59), sur le
     projet de finances pour 1982, adopté par l'Assemblée
     Nationale. Tomes I, II. November 23, 1981.

Sénat.   Commission des Affaires Culturelles.   _Avis_.   (no. 59),
    sur le projet de loi de finances pour 1982, adopté par
    l'Assemblée Nationale, Tome I, "Culture," November 23, 1981.

Sénat.   Commission des Finances, du Controle Budgétaire et des
    Comptes Economiques de la Nation.   _Rapport Générale_   (no.
    95), sur le projet de loi de finances pour 1983, adopté par
    l'Assemblée Nationale. Tome III. November 22, 1982.

Sénat.   Commission des Finances, du Controle Budgétaire et Des
    Comptes Economiques de la Nation.   _Avis_ (no. 96), sur le
    projet de loi de finances pour 1983, adopté par l'Assemblée
    Nationale. Tomes I, II. November 22, 1982.

Sénat.   Commission des Finances, du Controle Budgétaire et des
    Comptes Economiques de la Nation.   _Avis_ (no. 97), sur le
    projet de loi de finances pour 1986, adopté par l'Assemblée
    Nationale. Tome I. November 21, 1985.

Sénat.   Commission des Finances, du Controle Budgétaire et des
    Comptes Economiqes de la Nation.   _Rapport Général_ (no. 96),
    sur le projet de loi de finances pour 1986, adopté par
    l'Assemblée Nationale. Annexe no. 7, "Culture." November 21,
    1985.

INTERVIEWS

Abirached, Robert. Director of Theater, Ministry of Culture.
    Paris, July 21, 1983; July 18, 1986.

Bataillon, Michel. Director, Théâtre National Populaire de
    Villeurbanne. Villeurbanne, June 24, 1983.

Benoist, Alain de. *Nouvelle Droite* philosopher; publisher
    Eléments. Paris, July 12, 1983.

Billon, Alain. Deputy, National Assembly (PS). Paris, June 21,
    1983.

Boulez, Pierre. Director, IRCAM. Paris, November 6, 1986.

de Brebisson, Guy. Researcher, Ministry of Culture--Service des
    Etudes et Recherches. Paris, July 8, 1983; July 17, 1986.

de Plunkett, Patrice. Cultural editor, *Le Figaro Magazine*.
    Paris, June 22, 1983.

Fleuret, Maurice. Director of Music, Ministry of Culture.
    Paris, August 18, 1983; July 10, 1986.

Lang, Jack. Minister of Culture, 1981-1986. Paris, July 15,
    1986.

Libourel, André. Cabinet of Minister of Culture. Paris, June
    21, 1983.

Mollard, Claude. Director, Delegation of Plastic Arts. Paris,
    July 29, 1986.

Musy, Jean. Director of Cultural Affairs for the City of Paris;
    former director, Ecole des Beaux Arts. Paris, July 20,
    1983; July 8, 1986.

Pesce, Rodolphe. Deputy, National Assembly (PS). Paris, June
    29, 1983.

Rigaud, Jacques. Founder, ADMICAL; President RTL. Paris, July
    10, 1986.

Index

About the Author

DAVID WACHTEL is a freelance journalist and writer.